DL 76

BOOK 2

Anatomy Academy
Respiration, Circulation & Digestion

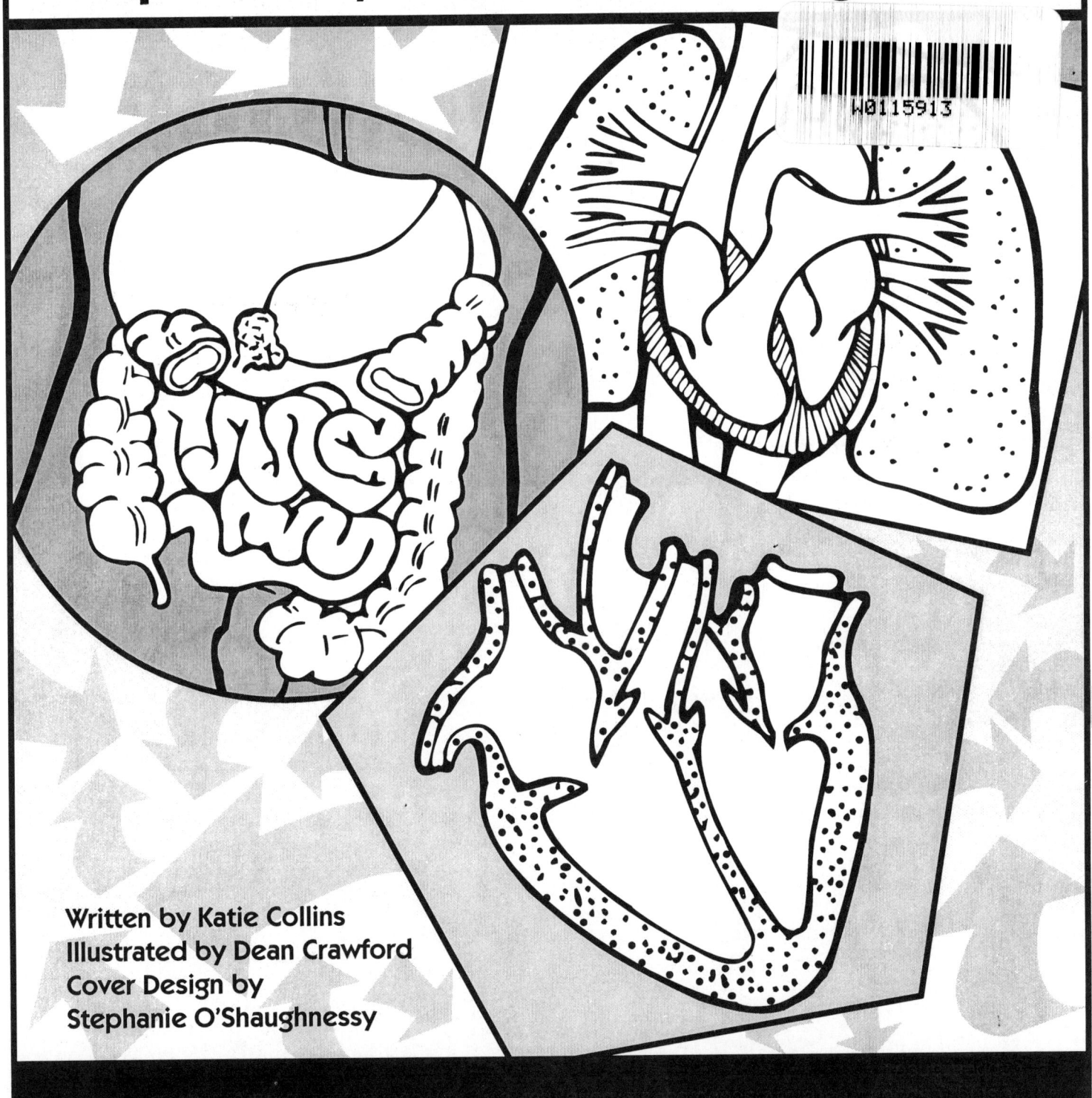

Written by Katie Collins
Illustrated by Dean Crawford
Cover Design by
Stephanie O'Shaughnessy

Table of Contents

Introduction

The body. Everyone has one, yet few understand its beauty and complex works. Its beauty lies in each individual cell, in its intricacy, and in the systems and functions these powerful cells create. To understand the body, we must look at each of these working parts separately to achieve a greater understanding of the body as a whole.

Anatomy Academy, a three-book series, invites you to discover the beauty and complexity of the human body. Each of the books focuses on three main topics. They cover the following topics:

Book 1 - Cells, Muscular System and Skeletal System

Book 2 - Respiratory, Circulatory and Digestive Systems

Book 3 - Nervous System, Senses and Glands.

The books are designed so that instructors will have a variety of teaching strategies and vehicles for learning and applying the information that is presented. Each topic is presented in six ways:

1. **Essential Information** - Informational pages filled with facts and fun. Review questions and activities are included at the bottom of each page. These may be used as teacher-directed material or as individual study sheets.

2. **Applying What You Know** - Activity pages designed to reinforce the information presented.

3. **Focus Pages** - Evaluation instruments that use a variety of questioning techniques.

4. **Discovery Experiments** - Instructions for experiments that can be used to demonstrate concepts, reinforce material presented, or develop analysis skills.

5. **Research Projects** - Ideas for research that provide opportunities for branching out into related areas, discovering relevant applications and implications, or pursuing individual interest.

6. **Special Projects** - Enrichment activities, including art projects, language arts activities, and various other projects that stimulate creativity and reinforce knowledge.

It is the purpose of the three *Anatomy Academy* books to unravel the beauty and complexity of the body. As students work through these activities, they should not only gain a considerable amount of knowledge about how their bodies work, but hopefully will develop an appreciation for the wonders of their bodies. In the end, they should be able to view their bodies as the most intricate, well-designed and incredible machines that have ever been produced.

It must be noted that as new discoveries are made, some of the material in this book may one day become outdated or revised. The thrust of scientific endeavors is to expand the realm of curiosity and to discover what has not yet been uncovered, to find more conclusive explanations, and to make more accurate measurements. Therefore, information may become outdated. How exciting! As you become actively involved with verifying information and offering hypotheses, you and your students will become participants in the ever-changing world of science.

The Circulatory System

Every cell in the body needs food and oxygen to survive. In order to meet the needs of all of these cells, we have a complex system that circulates a versatile fluid, blood, around the body in order to bring cells the nutrients they need to continue doing their various jobs. Without blood the body would be like a land whose inhabitants have no food, water, air, or any means of disposing of waste.

The **circulatory system** involves the movement of blood from the heart through arteries, capillaries and veins and back to the heart. The circulatory system performs several important jobs. It carries food, water, oxygen and wastes to and from all the cells in the body. The circulatory system includes the heart, blood, arteries, veins and capillaries.

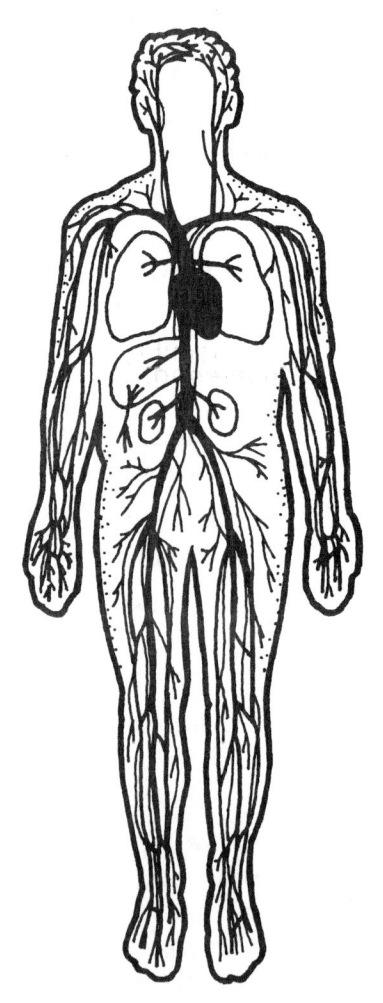

The biggest job the circulatory system does is the transportation of essential elements throughout the body. Nutrients taken from the food you eat, oxygen found in inhaled air, and antibodies and hormones are all carried to the cells in your body by the blood.

The heart pumps this blood through a complex network of vessels to every part of the body. Every living organ tissue and cell are provided with food and oxygen. Waste products, the non-usable things brought into the body, are also taken away from cells to their disposal sites by the blood. The waste products are taken to organs such as the liver, lungs and kidneys. Here, they are treated and expelled from the body.

Fact: The heart beats, circulating all of the blood through the body, more than 100,000 times per day.

Fact: The heart pumps a total of 5,000 to 6,000 quarts of blood through the body each day.

Something To Do

1. If you have 6 quarts of blood in your body how many pints, cups, and tablespoonfuls of blood are in your body?

2. List several important jobs the circulatory system does.

3. The word *circulatory* is derived from the word *circulate*. What does circulate mean? What does circuit mean? How do these words relate to the circulatory system?

4. If the heart beats about 100,000 times per day, how many times does it beat per minute?

It's Just Blood

People tend to have all sorts of reactions when they see blood, especially when it is their own. Taking a closer look, you will find that blood is an incredible liquid that flows through the body, carrying nutrients and chemicals to all the cells in the body. Blood contains red blood cells, white blood cells, plasma and platelets. About half of blood is a liquid called plasma. The other half is specialized cells (red, white and platelets), all of which perform different roles. Blood plays and important role in every bodily activity. It is the body's main system of transportation; a way to move various elements around to various parts of the body.

Infants are born with less than a quart of blood. An adult has between 6 and 10 quarts of blood. The exact amount of blood depends on body size and weight. The total supply of blood is in the circulatory system. There is, however, a backup supply of red blood cells stored in the liver and spleen that can be released when needed. There are no extra white blood cells, but when the body needs them, it can manufacture them quickly.

Blood performs several important jobs for the body. Some of these jobs are:

1. Red blood cells carry oxygen from the lungs to cells and carbon dioxide from the cells to the lungs where it can be exhaled.
2. Plasma transports antibodies that protect the body from infection.
3. The blood picks up dissolved food from the intestines and carries it to all cells that use it for energy.
4. It takes waste products out of the kidneys for disposal.
5. Blood transports hormones from glands to where they are needed in the body for sending chemical signals to tissues.
6. Clotting factors in the plasma prevent excessive blood loss when blood vessels are damaged.
7. It regulates the water content in tissue cells.
8. It equalizes body temperature by carrying heat from one part of the body to another.

Something To Do

1. **Hemat-** is a root word meaning blood. Make a list of other words that have been derived from this root word. Give a definition for each word.
2. List at least four of the main jobs that blood does. Underline a key word (or two) for each thing you list.
3. Press upwards on a fingernail with the thumb on your other hand. Watch your flesh under the nail turn white as you squeeze all the blood from its capillaries. Stop pressing your nail. Watch the original color return as the blood returns.

Oxygen Carriers

One of the most important elements of blood is the **red blood cells**. These cells are responsible for transporting oxygen to all the cells of the body and taking the waste product, carbon dioxide, from cells to the lungs where the blood cells can exchange carbon dioxide for oxygen and it can be exhaled from the body.

Red blood cells are formed in the marrow of some bones; mainly in the skull, spine, ribs, breastbone, and thighs. Soon after formation they lose their nuclei and become envelopes of **hemoglobin**. Hemoglobin is a protein made partly of **iron**. This is what gives the blood its red color. Hemoglobin combines easily with oxygen, so it is primarily responsible for the transfer of oxygen and carbon dioxide that takes place both in the lungs and in all the cells. Every cell needs oxygen, and red cells are an efficient means for a speedy and safe delivery.

Red blood cells are disk shaped and do not have a nucleus like other cells. Because red blood cells do not have a nucleus, they cannot reproduce like other cells can. The cells live for about 120 days and then they die. During this brief life, a red blood cell will travel about 1,000 miles through the circulatory system. New red blood cells are constantly being produced, however, in the spongy marrow of the larger bones. There are about two million new red blood cells being produced each second to replace the number that die. There are a total of about 5 million red blood cells in each cubic millimeter of blood. They are a thousand times more numerous than the white blood cells. People who live in higher altitudes usually will have more red blood cells. Because the air is thin (therefore contains less oxygen) they need extra red cells in order to get all the oxygen they need.

Something To Do

1. Explain why hemoglobin is important.
2. How are red blood cells different from white blood cells?
3. Write an obituary for a red blood cell.
4. Underline five key concepts to remember about red blood cells.

To The Rescue

Besides red cells, the other common cell in blood is the **white blood cell**. This cell is the body's defense against infection and poison. There are actually three different kinds of white blood cells (granulocytes, lymphocytes, and monocytes), each with a different job to perform in protecting the body against infection.

White cells are larger, sometimes twice as large as red cells. White cells are not as numerous as red cells, however. For every one white blood cell there are between 500 to 1,000 red blood cells. White cells are produced in bone marrow and also in other parts of the body, primarily the lymph system. They have no color and no real shape. They live for only 13 to 20 days. New cells are continually being produced to replace older ones.

White cells may live a shorter life than red cells, but the job they carry out during that lifetime is an extremely vital one. It is the function of a white blood cell to attack harmful bacteria or viruses that enter the body. The bacteria or virus may enter through the air that is breathed in, through a break in the skin, or even from contaminated food and water.

When one of these disease organisms enters the body, white cells bring out their secret weapon, the immune system. Antibodies are quickly produced to combat the virus or bacteria. Antibodies are produced in the lymph system. Lymph vessels spread to almost every part of the body, making a vast network of disease-fighting cells. A body can produce several kinds of antibodies to combat all kinds of diseases. Antibodies fight infection in three ways. They cause the invading organisms to clump together, they quickly latch onto the surface of special white cells called lymphocytes. These cells remember which disease they are designed to destroy, so when this organism enters the body, they multiply and grow rapidly. Once caught, the disease organism is destroyed. The immune system is on alert at all times, its white blood cells ready to fight the germs that can cause the body harm.

Something To Do

1. Underline six key points in the information above.
2. Discover how inoculations make your body immune to specific diseases.
3. Create a comic strip illustrating white blood cells at work. Make a white cell the hero or heroine.

Plasma Plus Platelets

Without plasma, red and white blood cells could never travel to where they are needed. Plasma is the yellowish liquid in blood that makes cell transportation possible. Plasma is ninety percent water, but suspended in it are blood cells, salts, hormones, vitamins, food nutrients, and proteins. It is constantly changing, gaining and losing chemical substances. Plasma is similar to fluid found in the tissues of the body and around cells in other parts of the body. It accounts for over half of the volume of the blood that flows through the body.

Plasma carries red and white blood cells and also tiny bits of cells called **platelets**. These cell bits have been broken off from larger cells found in the bone marrow. These cell pieces are smaller than the white blood cells and are forty times more numerous than white cells.

A platelet lives for only four to eight days but does an extremely important job. Platelets help blood to clot. They contain a chemical that is released at the site of an injury to assist in the initial stages of blood clotting when blood vessels are damaged. They clump together around a wound on the body's surface, trapping the red and white cells so they cannot escape. The platelets seal the cut while the body begins to repair itself. This seal is called a scab.

Scabs are seen on the surface of the skin. Bruises are the work of platelets doing their job under the skin. The capillaries in the body are injured when you fall or hit something hard. Although your skin was not cut, you still damaged the tissue underneath the skin. The black and blue mark that appears as a bruise indicates that blood vessels beneath the skin have been broken. Platelets go to work, clotting the blood under the skin as well as on the surface. In a sense, a bruise is a scab under the skin.

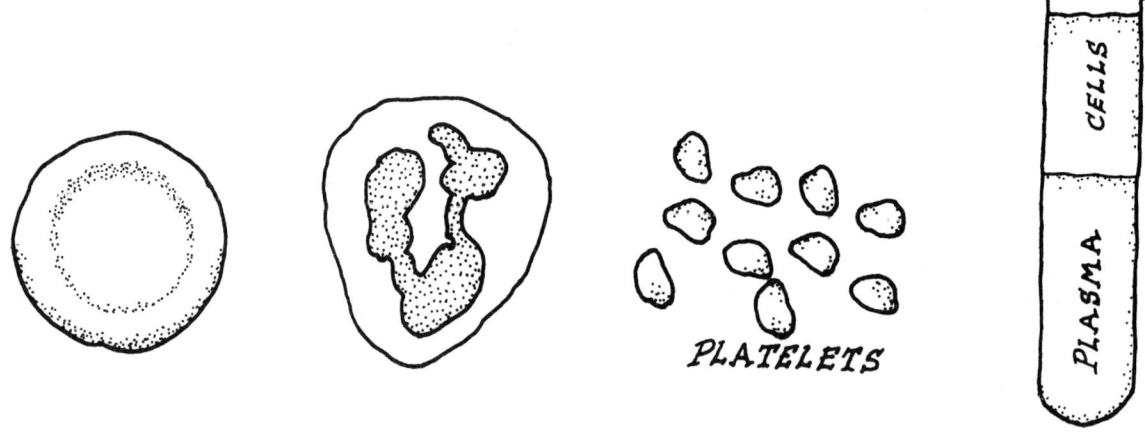

PLATELETS CELLS PLASMA

Something To Do
1. Outline the four components of blood. Provide at least three statements under each heading.
2. Write five questions concerning plasma, platelets, red blood cells and white blood cells.
3. Compose a riddle about each of the four components of your blood.
4. Find the meaning of **hemorrhage**.

Power Pump

Every fine piece of machinery has a main source of power. The power source in your body is your heart. Basically a pump, the heart pushes blood through the body one push after another, day in and day out. It begins to work during the fourth week of fetal development and continues throughout a person's entire life. During the course of a day, it pumps about 2,000 gallons of blood. A newborn baby's heart beats about 140 times a minute. An adult's heart beats 70 to 80 times a minute (or over 100,000 times a day), but this rate can be doubled with heavy exertion or stress.

The heart is located in the middle of the chest between the lungs. It is about the size and shape as a fist and weighs a little less than a pound. It tilts and points slightly over the left side of the body and is surrounded and protected by the ribs and the hard breastbone at the front of the chest. It has a very workable, powerful design that enables it to pump blood throughout the body.

The heart is like a tough, rubber balloon. It is hollow inside, and made out of a thick, sturdy muscle that is able to endure a constant and mighty pumping action. The heart is made of special muscles (**cardiac muscles**) that keep it working all the time. Most of the body's other muscles get tired after continuous use, but not the heart. A heart muscle will work tirelessly every day and does not need to take a rest except the momentary rest it takes between beats. No other muscle in the body works as hard as the heart muscle. Because it does so much work, it requires about ten times the nourishment of other tissues. It, therefore, requires a large supply of blood for its cells. It uses about 1/20 the body's supply of blood.

The heart has a built in rhythm of contractions. The **pacemaker** is a small area of specialized nerve tissue in the heart. The pacemaker makes sure that the chambers of the heart work in a coordinated way. It receives messages from the brain and, in turn, sends impulses of electricity through the walls of the heart causing them to contract, and this forces blood out of the heart. It keeps the heart beating at its 70 beats per minute rate. Without the pacemaker, the heart would beat about 40 times per minute. This would not be fast enough to satisfy the body's need for oxygen.

Something To Do

1. Underline the most important facts or concepts in each paragraph. Be prepared to explain why you think these are the most important.

2. Write a physical description of the heart.

3. Why does the heart need a greater amount of nourishment than other muscles?

Heart Parts

If your circulatory system is a transportation system, the heart is the powerhouse of that system. The heart is a pump that is designed to circulate blood in a way that allows it to pick up and drop off its cargo in every cell in the body. There are four chambers in the heart and blood flows in a figure-eight pattern with the heart at the center. During one heartbeat oxygenated blood enters the left side of the heart from the lungs and then is sent out to all parts of the body, while deoxygenated blood is received from the body into the right side of the heart and then sent to the lungs so the carbon dioxide can be traded for oxygen.

The heart contains four rooms, or **chambers**. Two of the chambers receive blood, while the other two pump it out into other parts of the body. A thick wall, called the **septum**, divides the heart down the middle. The two top chambers receive the blood that is returning to the heart either from the lungs or the body. They are called the left **atrium** and the right **atrium**. The atria can be thought of as holding chambers where blood is contained before it flows into the two bottom chambers. The right atrium receives blood from the body that contains carbon dioxide, while the left atrium receives blood from the lungs that contains oxygen.

The two bottom chambers are called the left **ventricle** and the right **ventricle**. They are much stronger and more muscular than the two atria on top. The ventricles have a bigger job to do. They pump blood out of the heart. They can be thought of as the pumping centers. The right ventricle pumps blood to the lungs, while the left ventricle pumps blood all over the body.

An important feature that allows the heart to work like a pump and makes sure blood moves in one direction is the valves in the heart. These valves close if blood attempts to move against its proper direction. It is the opening and closing of the valves that makes the lup-dub sound typically associated with the heart.

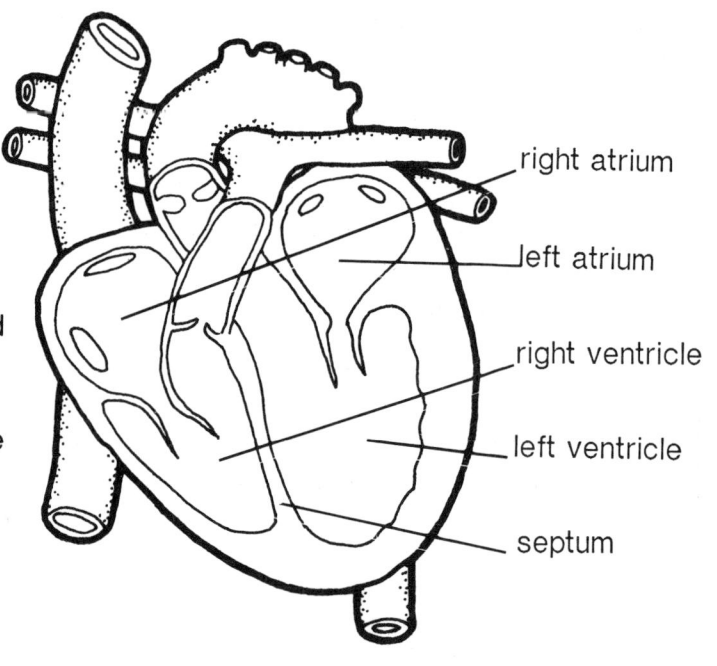

right atrium

left atrium

right ventricle

left ventricle

septum

Something To Do

1. Make a diagram that shows the inside of the heart and its four chambers. Label the parts.

2. Make a webbing of facts you have learned about the heart. Place the word heart in the center of your paper. Surround it with facts describing its structure and duties.

3. Choose five terms as answers to questions. Give the terms to a friend who will then invent five questions to go along with the answers.

All Around the Body

The heart performs a constant and powerful task as it pumps blood through the body's network of blood vessels. To begin the trip, the right ventricle pumps blood to the lungs where it picks up some fresh oxygen and rids itself of the useless carbon dioxide. Next, this oxygen-rich blood enters the left atrium, one of the top chambers of the heart. Then it travels down to the left ventricle, where it is forced out to every part of your body.

After a trip around the body where blood picks up food nutrients in the intestine and carries this food along with the oxygen from the lungs to all the cells where it exchanges the food and oxygen for wastes, blood comes back to the heart. On its return, it is filled with carbon dioxide. It then enters the right atrium and is squeezed through a one-way valve to the right ventricle below where it is pumped to the lungs. At this point it has completed the entire circuit.

The blood keeps moving in this way constantly. It only moves in one direction. It is a one-way system, because it needs to keep the fresh oxygen-carrying blood separate from the blood carrying carbon dioxide. Tiny flaps, or valves, inside the heart and inside the walls of the blood vessels, keep the blood flowing in one direction.

Blood travels from the heart to the lungs, back to the heart, all through the body, and then back to the heart once again. It begins its trip with fresh blood, but by the time it finally returns to the heart, the oxygen has all been used up. So, the trip begins all over again.

The route blood takes as it circulates through the heart is the following:

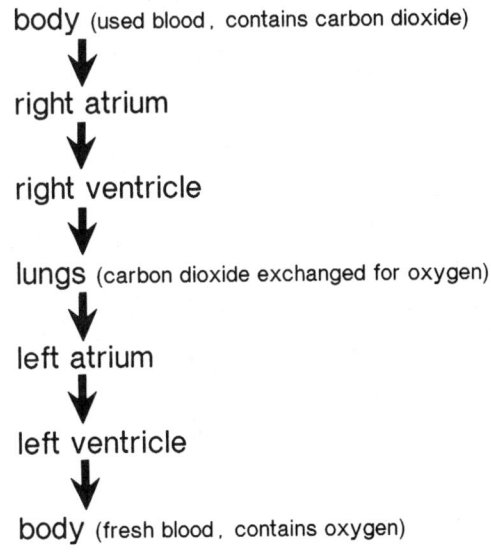

body (used blood, contains carbon dioxide)
↓
right atrium
↓
right ventricle
↓
lungs (carbon dioxide exchanged for oxygen)
↓
left atrium
↓
left ventricle
↓
body (fresh blood, contains oxygen)

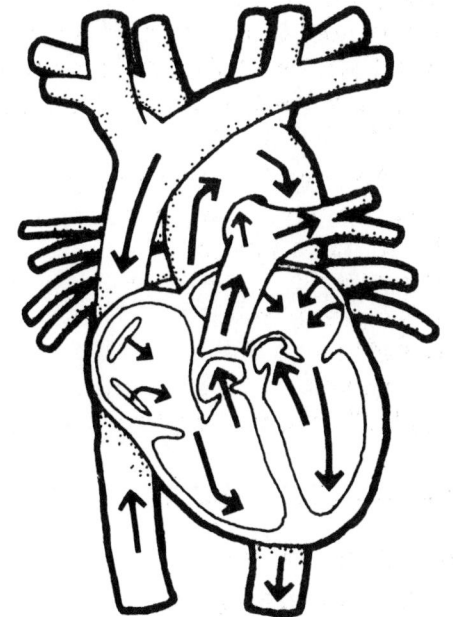

Something To Do

1. If blood travels about 61,320 miles in one year, how far does it travel in one day?

2. Blood travels the same way each trip through your body. Outline this systematic journey and tell what happens at each point. Begin with the blood being pumped to your lungs by the right ventricle.

Blood Vessels

Just as there are narrow side streets, two-lane roads, and major expressways for our cars to travel on, there are different types of tubes carrying blood to all parts of the body. As blood travels around the body, it travels in three major types of blood vessels called **veins**, **arteries**, and **capillaries**.

On its journey away from the heart, blood travels in major expressways called **arteries**. These arteries are the largest of the blood vessels. They are built with strong walls to receive and control large amounts of blood being circulated at a powerful pace with every beat of the heart. Blood in the arteries is under high pressure, so they are able to yield slightly with each surge of pressure from each of the heart's contractions. This slight expansion is your pulse.

The largest artery is called the **aorta**. It is nearly 1 inch in diameter. It runs out of the left ventricle of the heart, travels down the front of the spine, and branches out to supply blood to all parts of the body. It carries most of the blood being pumped away from the heart.

Arteries branch into smaller vessels called **arterioles** and then into the very smallest tubes, the narrow side streets of your body, called **capillaries**. The walls of capillaries are only one cell wide. They are incredibly thin; fifty times thinner than a piece of human hair. Capillaries are found all over the body. They comprise a huge network of tiny vessels that find their way to every spot in the body. It is only in these capillaries that oxygen and food can pass through the walls and travel to each cell in the body.

Once the blood in capillaries exchanges oxygen and other materials for carbon dioxide and waste from all of the cells, it drains into **venules** and then into larger tubes called **veins**. Veins take blood back to the heart. To make sure the blood continues to flow back to the heart, tiny valves found along the inside walls will close if the blood starts to flow backwards. Veins have thinner walls than arteries and are able to expand and collapse to adjust to different volumes of blood moving through them. The **superior vena cava** and **inferior vena cava** are two of the more important veins that return blood from the body back to the heart.

Blood Route

heart ➡ arteries ➡ capillaries ➡ veins ➡ heart ➡ lung ➡ heart

Something To Do

1. If you took all of the blood vessels in the body and laid them out end to end, they would measure about 60,000 to 70,000 miles. Using various kinds of reference books find three examples of a 60,000 to 70,000 mile distance.

2. Make a list of all the main arteries, veins and valves connected to the heart. Find out more about each one and the role it plays in the circulatory system.

3. Find out about arteriosclerosis and its relation to cholesterol. Tell why this condition is harmful.

Lub-Dub, Lub-Dub

"Lub-dub, lub-dub, lub-dub." What you are hearing is not your heart beating, but the small valves inside the heart that keep the blood flowing in one direction opening and closing. These valves close after each push of blood. With each push, or beat, of the heart, blood surges through the body's blood vessels. The blood vessels close to your skin's surface enable you to feel this pushing of blood through your body. This is called your **pulse**.

Pulse rate (the number of times your heart beats per minute) is not the same throughout your whole life. It changes as you change. It becomes slower as you get older. A newborn infant's heart could beat between 110-140 beats per minute. A child's pulse rate ranges from 90-120 beats per minute; and in an adult, it averages around 70 beats per minute. Each heart beat actually has three stages. The first stage is the contraction of the two atria. The second stage is the contraction of the two ventricles, and the last stage is a rest period.

The heart is able to speed up and slow down according to different needs of the body. The autonomic nervous system controls the heart, adjusting the output of blood to different situations. When the body is working hard, so is the heart. An increase in the body's activity causes the heart to beat faster, bringing oxygen and nutrients to the body's cells at a faster pace. When you are doing something like running or jumping, your heart needs to beat faster to send the blood to the muscle cells more quickly. The heart can respond to emotional stimuli the same way it responds to physical exertion. When you are nervous, surprised or scared, your heart may begin to race. This is all done automatically, without you having to think about it.

Something To Do
Feel your pulse. Find an artery close to the skin, like at the wrist. Place your fingertips on the inside of the wrist on the side closest to the thumb. Count your pulse (heart beats) for 1 minute while sitting down. This is your resting pulse.

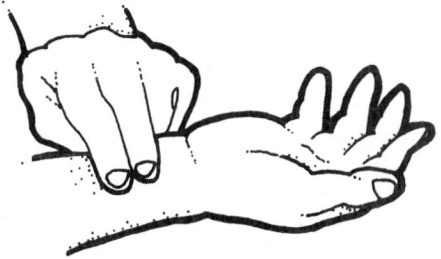

Perform the following activities. Check your pulse for one minute after each activity. Graph the results. Make sure to give yourself some rest or recovery time between each activity. Activities: a) lying down, b) sitting, c) standing, d) running for one minute, e) jumping rope for one minute.

Heart Work

The heart pumps about 2,500,000,000,000 times during a lifetime. Keeping your heart strong and healthy will keep you strong and healthy too. There are several things you can do to keep your heart healthy; like eating proper foods, getting exercise, and reducing high blood pressure.

Like any muscle, the heart will benefit from exercise. It will become stronger and larger as it is used more often. Most athletes live longer lives than those who chose not to exercise their bodies. By exercising, their hearts became strong enough to do the same amount of pumping work with fewer beats. They are able to spread those 2,500,000,000,000 lifetime pumps over a longer period of time, so they live longer.

Being active is an important way of keeping you and your heart healthy. Here is a list of extremely low pulse rates that trained athletes have achieved. These are resting pulse rates. These show just what exercise can do for a body.

athlete	beats per minute
average person	72
fencer	68
weight lifter	65
volleyball player	60
sprinter	58
football player	55
oarsman	50
swimmer	40
distance runner	35

In addition to getting adequate exercise, your heart will remain healthy if you restrain from smoking, eat a low fat/low cholesterol diet, and keep your weight within a normal range. True, there are some diseases or conditions that damage the heart that you have no control over, but everyone can provide basic good health for their heart by following the simple, accepted guidelines for diet and exercise.

Something To Do

1. In the chart above, you will notice that various sports develop the heart differently. State your hypothesis as to why a weight lifter's heart rate is greater than a swimmer's and a sprinter's heart rate is greater than a long distance runner's.

2. Underline three important concepts in the information above.

3. Give yourself and your family a grade for each of the following factors that contribute to good heart health: a) low fat diet b) no smoking c) normal weight d) exercise. If you did not rate well, make a plan for improvement.

4. Try this experiment to see how much work your heart does. Get a tennis ball and squeeze and release it continuously at the rate of seventy times per minute for as long as you can. Describe what happens.

Name _____

A Broken Heart

Directions: Read the sentence in each puzzle piece. Fill in the blanks with one of the missing words. Cut out the puzzle pieces and glue them onto another piece of paper in the shape of a heart.

Missing Words
cell	clot	one	oxygen
pumping	muscles	heart	fight

The heart is made of four chambers: two receiving blood and two pumping it out to the body. Valves maintain the flow of blood in _____ direction.

White blood cells _____ off infections and poison.

Plasma carries red and white blood cells and platelets. Platelets help blood to _____

Red blood cells transport oxygen to every cell in the body, take the carbon dioxide to the lungs where it is exchanged for more _____ .

The biggest job the circulatory system does is transport essential elements to every _____ in the body.

The power source in the body is the heart. Sturdy _____ keep it pumping without stopping.

Arteries carry the blood away from the heart. Capillaries are the tiniest blood vessels. Veins take blood back to the _____

The heart beats over 100,000 times per day, _____ over 5,000 quarts of blood.

Examining Marrow

Materials
large soup bones from a butcher (shin bones work well) sawed in half, microscope, glass slides, tweezers, spoon, paper towel, eyedropper, Benzidine-Nitroprusside

Procedure

1. Examine the bone as a whole. Identify the calcified bone at the surface, the spongy bone underneath, and the marrow in the center.

2. Separate the halves. Examine the inside of the bone filled with bone marrow. This is where all of the red blood cells are produced.

3. If the bone is fresh, you will be able to discover where the blood vessels enter the bone. Pull away the periosteum, or the cover skin, of the bone. The small red dots you see are the entryways for blood vessels.

4. Using a spoon, carefully scoop out the bone marrow. Investigate its texture and appearance.

5. Using tweezers, place a small portion of the marrow onto a clean glass slide.

6. Drop a drop of benzidine-nitroprusside onto the marrow. Cover with another slide.

7. Examine the cells under the microscope.

8. Draw what you see.

Dissection

Examine a heart. A lamb's heart works well. Its structure is similar to that of a human heart. Try to find one that has not been trimmed or split open.

Materials
lamb heart, long sharp knife, paper towels

Procedure

1. Lay the heart on its back.

2. Locate some of the main blood vessels. Locate the aorta, pulmonary artery, and veins leading from the lungs. You may need to tear off some fat.

3. Using a long, sharp knife, slice the heart in half. Cut slowly and carefully lengthwise.

4. Locate the four chambers of the heart, the valves, the main arteries, and the veins.

Examining the Mouth

There is a lot more in your mouth than left over peanut butter and jelly sandwich crumbs.
Take a look under your tongue to discover all the blood vessels living there.

Materials
mirror, flash light, magnifying glass (optional)

Procedure
1. Look into a mirror. Open your mouth and lift your tongue. Shine a bright light into your mouth.
2. Identify the following vessels:
    a) Thin blue lines – veins carrying blood back to your heart.
    b) Thick pink lines – arteries coming from the heart.
    c) Tiny, very thin lines – capillaries carrying food and oxygen to cells.

Blood Types

Materials
sterile lancets, sterile cotton, alcohol, toothpicks, blood typing serum (anti-A and anti-B), wax pencil, microscope slide, microscope

Procedure
1. Divide microscope slide in half with a wax pencil. Label the left side anti-A and the right anti-B.
2. Put one drop of anti-A serum on the left side of the slide and one drop of anti-B serum on the right side of the slide.
3. Clean the tip of your finger with a swab of alcohol. Pierce the tip with the lancet. Do not use the lancet more than once or share with another student.
4. Put one drop on each side of the slide near the drop of serum. Do not touch the serum.
5. Working quickly so the blood does not clot, mix blood with the serum with a toothpick. Use a different toothpick for each serum.
6. After one minute examine each slide under a microscope for clumping of cells, called **agglutination**. Compare results with the description below.

    Agglutination in anti-A only – blood type A

    Agglutination in anti-B only – blood type B

    Agglutination in both – blood type AB

    No agglutination – blood type O

Something's Fishy

Examine a goldfish tail to see the flow of blood through its capillaries.

Materials

live goldfish, gauze, fish net or cup, water, scissors, glass slide, aquarium or fish bowl, microscope

Procedure

1. Soak a piece of gauze in water.
2. Gently capture the goldfish. Wrap it carefully in the wet gauze. Be sure to cover the gills so they remain moist.
3. Place the wrapped fish lengthwise across the glass slide.
4. Loosen the gauze to gently free the back tail fin. Spread the fin across the slide.
5. Place the slide on the microscope stage. Focus the microscope on the tail's capillaries. Observe the flow of blood, one blood cell at a time.
6. Replenish the gauze with a small amount of water from a cup when needed. Try not to let any water drip onto the glass slide.
7. When finished observing, unwrap the goldfish. Place it back into its bowl.

Blood

Examine your blood closely with this experiment.

Materials

microscope, cotton ball, glass slides, methyl alcohol, cover glass, Wright's stain, needle, beaker or small jar, match

Procedure

1. Hold the tip of the needle in a flame for a few seconds to sterilize it.
2. Wash the tip of one of your fingers with a cotton ball of alcohol. Rub that finger upwards to force the blood to the tip.
3. Stick the tip of the needle into your fingertip so that a drop of blood forms.
4. Put the drop of blood on a slide and use another slide to spread the drop into a thin smear. Let the blood dry for a few minutes.
5. Place a drop of Wright's stain on the smear. When the smear changes to a pink color, rinse the slide in a beaker or small jar of water.
6. Put a cover slide over the smear.
7. Examine the smear. Locate the following: a) red blood cells (look like tiny doughnuts), b) white blood cells (no real shape, almost completely transparent), c) platelets (probably too small for you to see).

1. Blood Types

People have different types of blood. It is important to know your blood type if you ever need to receive or give blood. Find out more about the four main blood types, donating blood, Karl Landsteiner (the scientist who developed the ABO system of blood groups), and the RH factor.

2. Lymph System

Some things floating around in your body are just too big to get where they need to go. Your lymph system aids in the transportation of these larger particles. Find out more about the function of the lymph system.

3. Heart Facts

Write to the American Heart Association. Obtain as much information as you can concerning the heart and problems of the heart. Use the information to write a plan for a healthy heart.

4. Blood Disease

Leukemia is a serious blood disease. Find out more about this disorder and what medical breakthroughs are being made to treat and conquer this deadly disease.

5. E.K.G.

What is an electrocardiogram? Why is it used and what does it show?

6. Heart Disease

Find out about some of these common problems with the heart: rheumatic fever, thrombosis, stroke, heart attack, or arteriosclerosis. Report on the cause, effect, and cure.

7. Hemophilia

One blood disease that can be passed down through the family, generation after generation, is hemophilia. Discover what this disease means to its victims. Investigate the plight of the Russian royal family and their struggle with hemophilia.

8. Blood Pressure

Research high blood pressure (hypertension), its causes, and the problems related to it.

9. Bloodletting

Delve into the past to discover the original meaning behind the red and white striped pole posted outside a barbershop.

10. Anemia

Define anemia. Give the symptoms of someone who is anemic. What can be done to overcome this disorder?

11. Heart Song

Does your heart sing? Find out more about heart murmurs; why they occur, and what effect they have on the individual.

12. Stop!

A blockage within the body anywhere means trouble. Your circulatory system needs to flow smoothly and continuously. Discover the effects a blockage in your circulatory system can have on your body. Your brain, heart and legs are the most serious locations for blockage.

1. Blood Types

There are four main blood types: A, B, AB, and O are the most common. Take a poll around your classroom, school, or neighborhood to determine the average percentage of people in each blood group. Display your results. Supply information defining the different blood groups for those observing the results of your poll.

2. Heart Attack

Heart attacks are serious, yet common health problems. Invite a trained nurse or paramedic to demonstrate the saving techniques for a heart attack victim. Videotape the presentation. Collect any material that may be provided by the speaker. Combine the material and tape into a learning kit for your school library. Create activities and questions to accompany the tape.

3. Blood Pressure

Blood is pumped through the body at an extremely powerful force. This force is blood pressure. Invite a nurse or physician in to explain blood pressure and take the blood pressure of classmates. Then graph the results using both systolic/diastolic pressure readings and determine the average blood pressure.

4. Heart Celebration

Celebrate a **Love Your Heart Day**. Offer informational packets on the heart for those attending your celebration. Decorate with visual displays concerning the heart. Provide heart warming goodies for all to enjoy.

5. Heart Shape

Construct a true-to-shape model of the heart. Use materials available to you such as modeling clay, paper mache, cardboard, elastic tubing, etc. Be creative with your materials, yet accurate with the design.

6. Word Time

Design a crossword puzzle or a word-find puzzle utilizing the key words from the circulatory system. Share with your friends.

7. Good For You

Create a collage of things you enjoy doing that are good for your heart (exercising, eating the right foods). Combine all of your illustrations into an imaginative shape associated with the circulatory system.

8. Game Time

Design a game board displaying the physical make-up of the circulatory system. Add questions to accompany the board that emphasize the information about the circulatory system.

9. Rolling and Circulating

Create a roller movie illustrating the circulation of blood through the body.

10. Band–Aid

The band-aid was invented to protect a wound from infection while it was healing. Modify the conventional band-aid with some ideas of your own. Before you start, think about:

- What is the purpose of a band-aid?
- Is the design effective?
- How can it be improved?

State your reasons for the changes needed.

11. Healthy Habits

Make a poster that tells people about some of the things they can do to maintain a healthy heart and circulatory system.

12. Teaching Others

Plan and present a lesson for younger students that will give them some basic information about the circulatory system. Include visual aids or charts. Rewrite the words to a song or rhyme to tell about the circulatory system. Teach it as part of your lesson.

Name _____

Focus Page

I. Read the definitions and descriptions in the right column. Find the word in the left column that matches the description in the right column. Write the correct letter on the blank next to each word.

____ 1. heart   a. smallest of the body's tubes carrying blood
____ 2. iron   b. do not have a nucleus
____ 3. septum   c. largest artery
____ 4. antibodies   d. pushing of blood through the body
____ 5. capillaries   e. fights foreign organisms and toxins
____ 6. ventricles   f. hemoglobin is composed partly of this mineral
____ 7. aorta   g. two bottom chambers of the heart
____ 8. red blood cells h. parts of blood that aid in clotting
____ 9. pulse   i. thick wall dividing heart down the middle
____ 10. platelets   j. made of cardiac muscle

II. Fill in the blanks with one of the words listed below.

transportation   infection   heart   receive   veins
hemoglobin   capillaries   supply   valves   needs

1. The heart requires one twentieth of the body's _____ of blood.
2. _____ is the carrier of oxygen in red blood cells.
3. The _____ begins pumping at one month of fetal development.
4. The top two heart chambers _____ blood returning to the heart.
5. _____ take blood back to the heart.
6. The biggest job of the circulatory system does is the _____ of essential elements throughout the body.
7. Oxygen passes through the walls of the _____ and enters the bloodstream to travel to all cells in the body.
8. _____ keep the blood flowing in one direction.
9. White blood cells protect the body against _____ .
10. The heart speeds up or slows down according to the _____ of the body.

Put your answers to these questions on a separate piece of paper.

III. Define the following terms.

chambers   pacemaker   plasma   pulse   blood cells

IV. Draw the following.
    a.   Make a diagram that shows the route blood takes as it travels in the heart.
    b.   Make a diagram that shows the different kinds of vessels blood travels through after it leaves the heart and moves through the body.

V. Answer the following questions in clear, concise sentences.
    a.   Give three examples of jobs that are performed by the blood in the body.
    b.   Compare and contrast red and white blood cells.
    c.   Explain the circulation of blood through the body. Begin at the right ventricle.
    d.   Identify and define the three different types of blood vessels.
    e.   Make a list of ideas for keeping your heart strong and healthy.

Reason For Breathing

Your body is an incredible piece of machinery — a factory of tissues, organs and systems that all work together in complicated, intricate ways. The cells need oxygen to survive. This oxygen is used by the cells to burn food to make energy. Air is breathed from the environment into the lungs to provide oxygen for all the cells. You could live without a television or one night's dinner, but you could not live for more than a few minutes without air.

Luckily for you, breathing is one of those jobs that is done automatically — you don't have to remember to fill-up on air. This breathing process, called **respiration**, goes on whether you are asleep or awake, resting or running. It is an **involuntary** process, because you don't have to think about it.

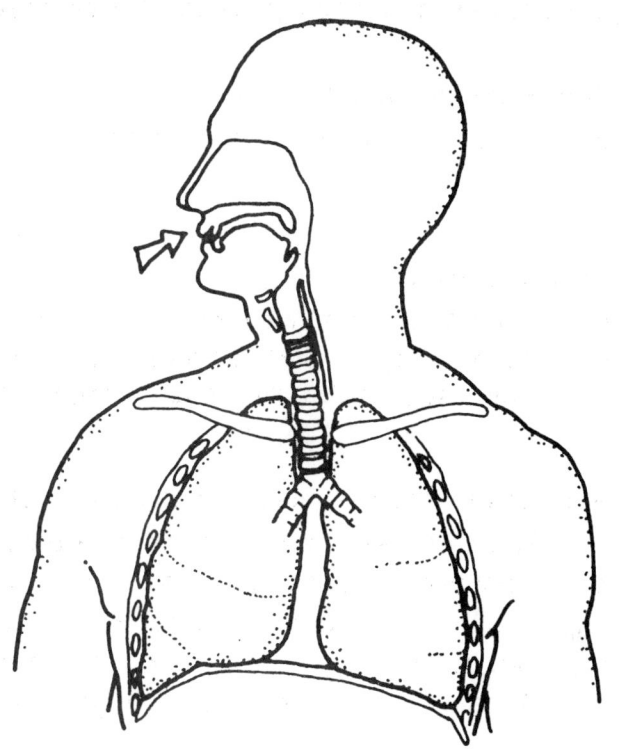

The purpose of the respiration system is to facilitate the exchange of gases in the lungs. The **respiratory center** is in the brain stem at the back of the brain. It controls all of the actions of the breathing process. It sends signals to the **diaphragm** telling it how quickly it needs to contract or relax to bring air into the lungs. It tells the heart to beat faster so it can bring the oxygen to the cells.

The level of carbon dioxide in the blood is the most important regulator of respiration. When the level is too high, a message is sent to the respiratory center in the brain. This respiratory center monitors the level of carbon dioxide and the acidity level in the blood. In response to a message saying the carbon dioxide level is too high, it is stimulated and sends a message to the muscles to inhale. The respiratory center responds quickly to changes in carbon dioxide in the blood. An increase of just 3/10 of a percent of carbon dioxide will double the volume of air breathed in and out.

But, as you have probably experienced, the signals from your respiratory center can be overridden within limits. You can control your breathing process for a short while if needed. For example, you control your breathing when you swim, pant, or hold your breath. For the most part, however, these breathing muscles perform on their own.

Something To Do

1. Discover your breathing rates for the following activities. Use the second hand of a watch or clock to time the number of breaths per minute you take: a) resting b) after two minutes of vigorous activity.

2. Describe in your own words why you begin to feel light-headed or dizzy when you hold your breath.

3. Be the respiratory center and describe why you are so important.

Respiration Basics

Respiration is not just breathing in and out. It is a complicated process that involves not just the respiratory system but is also linked to the circulatory system. Specifically, respiration is the process that involves the breathing movements of the lungs, the intake of oxygen, and the release of carbon dioxide. These things are linked to the biochemical processes that change energy in food into compounds that cells can use for their many functions.

The respiratory system does several things for the body. These are:

1. It brings oxygen into the body where it can be absorbed by the blood and used by all cells to produce energy.
2. It takes carbon dioxide from the blood and exhausts it to the outside.
3. It helps produce sound.
4. It maintains the balance of acid in the blood.

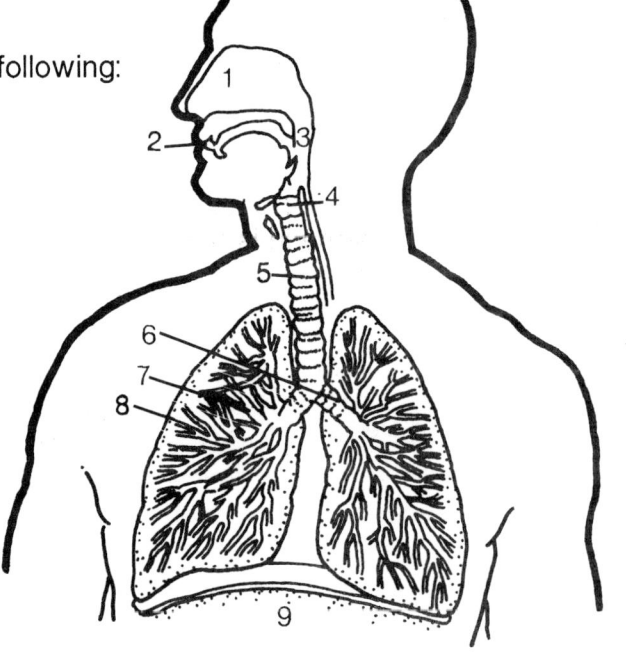

The main parts of the respiratory system are the following:

1. **Nasal cavity** (nose) – where air is taken into the body, warmed and moistened.
2. **Oral cavity** (mouth) – an additional air passage.
3. **Pharynx** (throat) – cavity behind the mouth and nose where air is further cleaned and moved into the trachea.
4. **Larynx** (voice box) – where vocal cords make sounds for speech.
5. **Trachea** (wind pipe) – tube that takes air to the lungs.
6. **Bronchi** – two tubes, one tube leads to each side of the lungs.
7. **Bronchioles** – smaller branches of the bronchi within the lungs, containing the air sacs called **alveoli**.
8. **Lungs** – two sponge-like organs, filled with capillaries and air sacs where the exchange of gases takes place.
9. **Diaphragm** – sheet-like muscle below the lungs that contracts and relaxes forcing air into and out of the lungs.

Something To Do

1. Pretend you are a cell and tell why the respiratory system is important to you.
2. Have a friend trace around the top part of your body. Draw in the main parts of the respiratory system. Label each part.
3. Name the four things the respiratory system does for the body.

The Air We Breathe

You have been breathing since the moment you were born; breathing automatically, each and every minute of every day. Each day you breathe about 5,000 gallons of air. Your body needs the oxygen in the air to release the energy that is locked up in food materials.

A baby takes about 40 breaths a minute, while an adult takes between 13 to 17 breaths per minute. This rate can be raised to as much as 80 breaths per minute with vigorous exercise. At an average rate of 15 breaths per minute, this would mean that you breathe more than 20,000 times per day. With each breath, you take in about 3/4 pint of air. During physical exertion the amount of air needed can be twenty times more than when you are resting. This means that not only does your rate of respiration increase but also the amount of air you breathe with each breath is greatly increased. When necessary, you can take in much more than the normal 3/4 pint per breath.

Of the air that is breathed in, only about 2/3 of it goes to the air sacs in the lungs to be used to restore the oxygen level in the blood. One third of the air stays in the bronchi. This means that the lungs are never completely drained of air. The lungs usually have between 1 1/2 to 2 1/2 pints of residual air in them.

Air is made up of several different gases, the most important being oxygen. Nitrogen and carbon dioxide are also found in air. The air you breathe in is not the same air you breathe out, because cells take oxygen out of the air and use it to turn the food into energy and, in exchange, give off waste products they don't need. The air we breathe out usually has about 4% less oxygen and 4% more carbon dioxide than the air we breathed in.

Gases In Air

	Inhaled	Exhaled
Nitrogen	79.02%	79.2%
Oxygen	20.94%	16.3%
Carbon Dioxide	0.04%	4.5%

Something To Do

1. Develop a hypothesis as to why a baby would need to take more breaths per minute than an adult.

2. Underline the three facts about the air you breathe (things you think are the most interesting).

3. Make a graph that shows the differences between and amounts of gases inhaled and exhaled.

4. Demonstrate the presence of carbon dioxide in exhaled air. Put a straw into a glass of lime water. Blow into the straw. The precipitate that forms is calcium carbonate, a substance formed from the chemical reaction of calcium in the lime and carbon dioxide.

The Nose

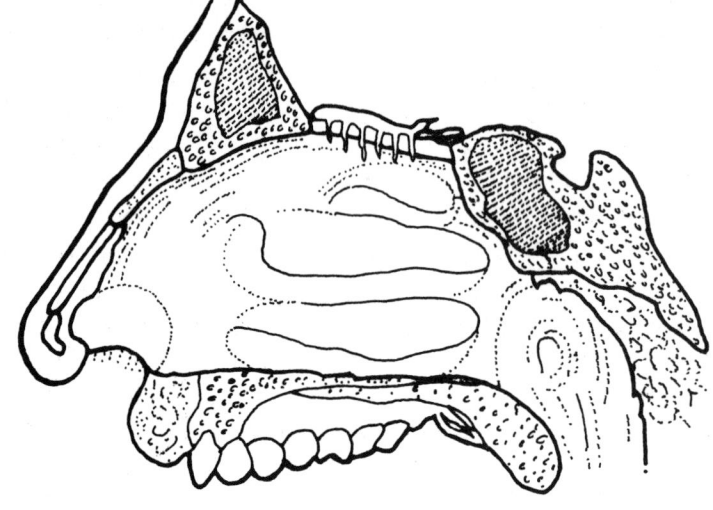

Respiration begins with your nose and mouth. You **inhale** through your nose or mouth, and you **exhale** also through your nose or mouth. The nose, the entrance mostly used, has a major role in the breathing process. The nose acts as the first filter for the incoming air. It cleans the air, warms it, and adds moisture to it. All this is done immediately after the air enters the nose. Because the nose does a much better job of warming, filtering and moistening air than the mouth, it is better to breathe through the nose than through the mouth.

The nose is an effective instrument for filtering and moistening the air that enters from the environment. It is lined with hairs that prevent foreign bodies from entering the body. It is also divided into a maze of passages by small bones. The passages are filled with tissue and glands that secrete **mucus**. Germs and bits of dust are trapped by this dampened material. The nose produces a new mucus layer about every 20 minutes to trap bacteria and particles. In addition to larger hairs and mucus, tiny hairs called **cilia** line the walls of the nose. Cilia move in a wavelike motion, carrying large and small pieces of dirt out of the air passages. Once enough dirt and germs have been collected by the mucus and cilia, they are disposed of by forcing them to the nose and mouth where they are either swallowed (and destroyed by digestive juices in the stomach), coughed up, or blown out with a sneeze.

Air is also warmed in the nose so that it is just the right temperature when it reaches the lungs. The nose has three bone chips that protrude from the side walls of the nostrils. These bones are covered with tissue that has a rich supply of blood. When air flows past this blood supply, it is warmed. The blood vessels in the nose can raise the temperature of the air from near freezing to almost body temperature by the time it reaches the back of the throat.

Something To Do

1. Underline three functions of the nose in the respiratory process.
2. Explain why it is better to breathe through the nose than through the mouth.
3. Develop a hypothesis about what effect nose shape (long, short, broad, thin) would have on the ability to warm, moisten, and clear air. Would certain noses be better suited to some climates or environments?
4. Develop a hypothesis explaining why your nose becomes pink when you are in cold weather.

It's an Open and Shut Case

You breathe in air through your nose or mouth, mainly through your nose. From your nose, air travels into your throat, or **pharynx**. From here the air travels into the **larynx**, into the **trachea**, and on to the lower parts of the respiratory system.

The **pharynx** is the cavity behind the nose and mouth, whose major function is to pick up and destroy bacteria trapped in the mucus film that coats the nasal cavity. This member of the respiratory system is coated with the same mucus and cilia cells found in the nose. Here too, the inhaled air is cleaned, warmed and moistened. When the pharynx has collected too much dirt and germs, it reacts automatically by coughing.

The throat links the mouth, nose, esophagus (leading to the stomach) and trachea (leading to the lungs). Travelling down the pharynx, the air enters a tube, the **trachea**. At the top of this tube is a small flap called the **epiglottis**. This lid opens and closes. It is open when the body is breathing and closed when swallowing to prevent food and liquid from entering the trachea. At this brief moment when swallowing takes place, breathing stops. This allows food to travel down the esophagus instead of down the trachea. If you try to both swallow and breathe at the same time, you may start to choke. When you attempt to do these two things at the same time, the epiglottis does not know whether to open or close.

If this has ever happened to you, you were probably able to cough your way out of this potential choking situation and return to eating your meal. A person who is in a serious choking situation cannot cough. The person cannot breathe in or out and cannot speak. This choking victim needs immediate help. Permanent brain damage or death can result in a matter of a few minutes. The choking victims can communicate that they are choking by using this widely accepted signal — they grasp their neck between the thumb and finger, saying in sign language that they are choking. The **Heimlich Maneuver** has proven to be a successful tool in saving a choking victim.

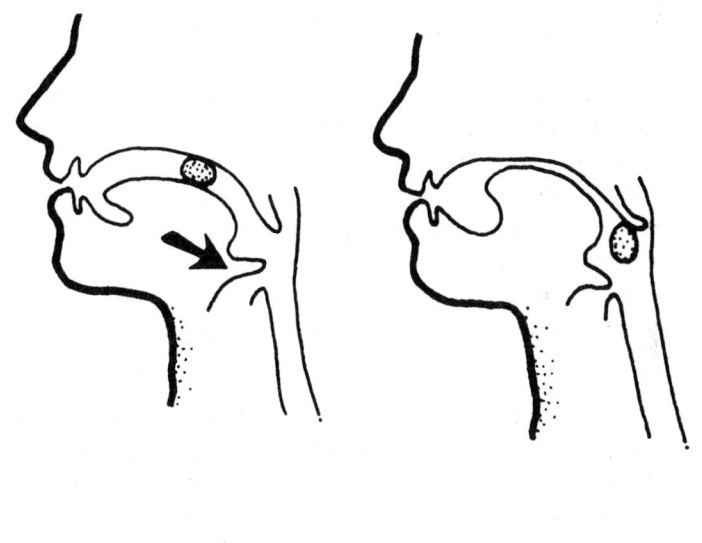

Something To Do

1. Research the Heimlich Maneuver. Find out what it is and how it is done.
2. Underline the key words on this page. Use them to write a brief summary of the information presented.
3. Illustrate the flow of air in a normal breathing situation and also as it would look in a choking situation.
4. Write a set of instructions for an epiglottis that would tell it how to do its job.

You Can Say That Again

Air travels from the nose to the pharynx and down a tube in the neck called the windpipe, or trachea. The trachea is a large, muscular tube that is kept in place by rings of cartilage. The trachea, like the nose, has cilia that move particles caught in mucus up and away from the lungs.

At the top of the trachea is the voice box, or larynx. It lies in the throat just below the chin and above the breastbone. The larynx is hollow, made out of cartilage, and has folds of tissue stretched across from front to back. These tissue folds are the vocal cords. Movement of expired air across these vocal cords produces sound in the following way:

1. Air is let out of the lungs.
2. The air passes through the windpipe, or trachea.
3. The vocal cords vibrate as the air rushes past them.
4. The vibrating vocal cords make sound waves in the surrounding air. By correctly using the lips, tongue and teeth, the sounds can be broken up into words.

The length and tightness of the vocal cords will determine how high or low the voice sounds. Vocal cords continue to grow for many years past the time when the rest of the body stops growing. With old age vocal cords begin to shorten, making the voice higher again. Also the faster air moves past the larynx, the louder will be the sound. In addition to the length of the vocal cords, the cavities of the mouth, nose, sinuses, throat and chest contribute to the quality and loudness of the voice. This is why everyone has their own individual intonations.

Vocal Cord Growth
(approximate lengths)

Age	Boys	Girls
Birth	2 1/2"	2 1/2"
age 2	3"	3"
age 6	4"	4"
age 14	5"	4 1/2"
age 20	10"	6 1/2"
age 30	12"	8"

Something To Do

1. Describe to a friend how expired air allows you to make a sound.
2. Try talking as you inhale and as you exhale. Which feels most natural?
3. Place your fingers over your larynx. Feel the vibrations as you speak. Do the vibrations feel different when you make high sounds than when you make low sounds?
4. Make a graph that shows the lengths of vocal cords at different ages.

The Great Exchange

Inhale, exhale, inhale, exhale, inhale. The air you have inhaled has entered through your nose or mouth, passed by your larynx, down the trachea and is now ready to enter your lungs. Each of the lungs is a sponge-like tissue that is interlaced with a network of capillaries. This is where the exchange of oxygen and carbon dioxide takes place.

After the trachea enters the chest area, it divides into two branches called **bronchial tubes**. The bronchi (meaning many tubes) are stiff. Cartilage rings protect them from hitting against each other while breathing. They expand when air is taken in and decrease in size as it is let out. The tubes are lined with cilia to rid the inhaled air of any dust that may have been inhaled.

Each bronchial tube divides into smaller and even smaller tubes as it enters the lung. They branch out like limbs on a tree, becoming like small twigs at the end of each tube. These smaller branches, called **bronchioles**, are about 2/100 of an inch in diameter and there are more than 250,000 of them.

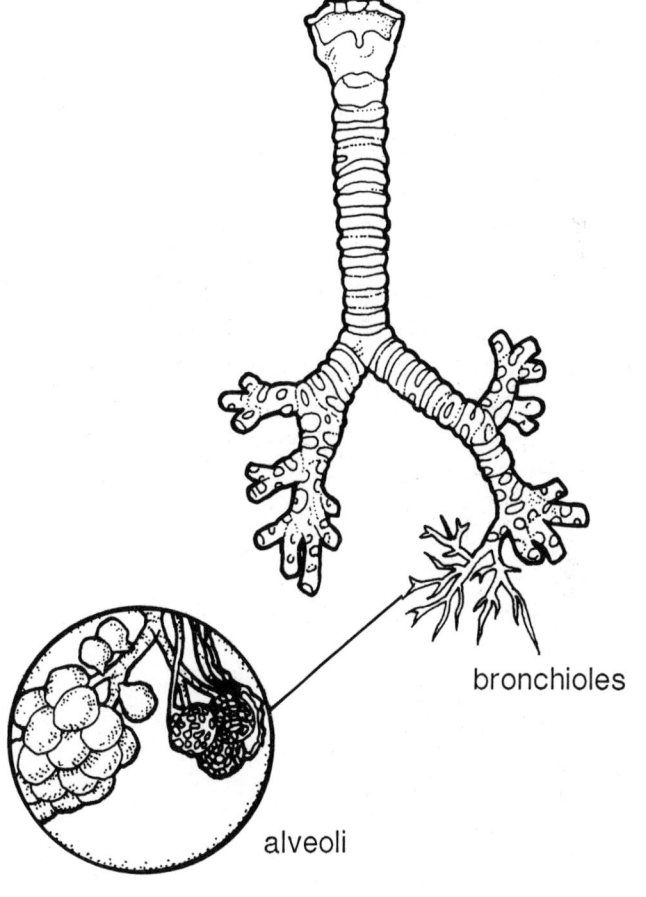

bronchioles

alveoli

At the end of each tiny tube are microscopic air sacs. The air sacs are called **alveoli**. There are nearly a billion air sacs found in the lungs. There are so many alveoli that if they were flattened out, they would cover half a tennis court. These sacs are hollow and clustered together like grapes. Each minuscule air sac has an extremely thin wall (one cell thick) around it, networked by numerous small capillaries, so small that only one blood cell can pass through at a time. The exchange of gases takes place across this barrier in a mere fraction of a second. The oxygen that entered the lungs is exchanged for the carbon dioxide in the blood, a waste product from cell metabolism. This fresh oxygen-carrying blood flows back to the heart and is then pumped throughout the entire body. The waste, carbon dioxide, is exhaled.

Something To Do

1. Describe the process by which gases are exchanged in the respiratory system. Make a drawing to show the route oxygen and carbon dioxide take.

2. The way bronchial tubes branch out is often compared to branches on a tree. What other comparison could be made?

3. State your theory about why oxygen is absorbed into the body in the air sacs rather than in the trachea or bronchial tubes.

The Chest Cavity

Lungs have no muscles of their own. The muscles that surround the chest cavity do most of the work during regular breathing. Specifically the muscles of the diaphragm and chest wall contract, causing expansion of the chest, and thus the lung tissue, causing air to be drawn into the nose or mouth. Expiration (breathing out) is usually just the relaxation of the muscles of the chest wall and diaphragm. The diaphragm, spine, and ribs form a protective shield around the chest cavity, the **thorax**. The two most vital organs, the heart and lungs, are located here.

Each of the lungs is enclosed in an airtight lining called a **pleural sac**. The pleura is actually two thin layers of connective tissue. One layer covers the outer lung, and the other layer covers the inner-chest wall. The pleural cavity is the space between these two layers. It is filled with a thin film of fluid that allows the forces created by the expansion of the chest wall and the diaphragm to fill the lungs with air.

The **diaphragm** is a muscular membrane that separates the organs of the chest (lungs and heart) from those of the abdomen and forces air into and out of the lungs. The diaphragm enables you to breathe air into and out of your lungs. By pulling together and moving downward, the muscles of the diaphragm let the ribs swing up and out as you inhale. Air can then travel down to the lungs. As you exhale, the diaphragm relaxes, allowing the ribs to come back down. Air can then escape through the nose or mouth. Breathing begins and ends with the diaphragm. The muscles of the diaphragm enable the lungs to bring air into the body so it can claim the oxygen it needs and get rid of the carbon dioxide it does not need. Without these muscles, the lungs could not do their important job.

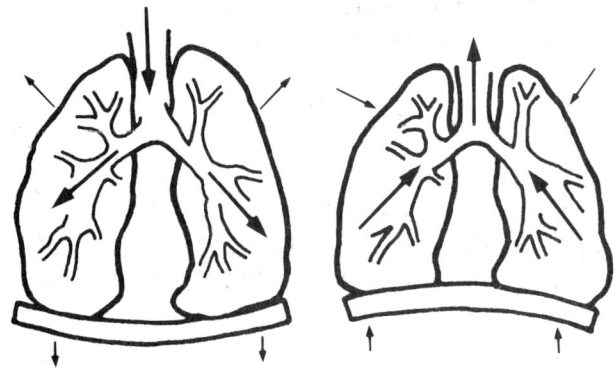

Something To Do

1. Describe in your own words the function of the diaphragm muscles.
2. Examine your diaphragm at work with this experiment. Breathe in and out naturally, paying close attention to the rise and fall of your chest. Try to breathe without moving your chest. Explain the job your diaphragm performs to a friend.
3. Diaphragm muscles are (voluntary, involuntary, cardiac) muscles. Explain your choice.
4. Demonstrate the flexibility of the chest cavity by measuring the distance around your ribs after inhaling and after exhaling. Explain the difference.

The Complete Breathing Process

You do lots of different things during your day, yet you continue to breathe without stopping and without thinking about breathing. The following is the complete breathing process:

The air is inhaled through the **nose** or **mouth** with the help of the **diaphragm** muscles that contract to cause the lungs to expand. It is warmed, moistened and cleansed of dirt and germs.

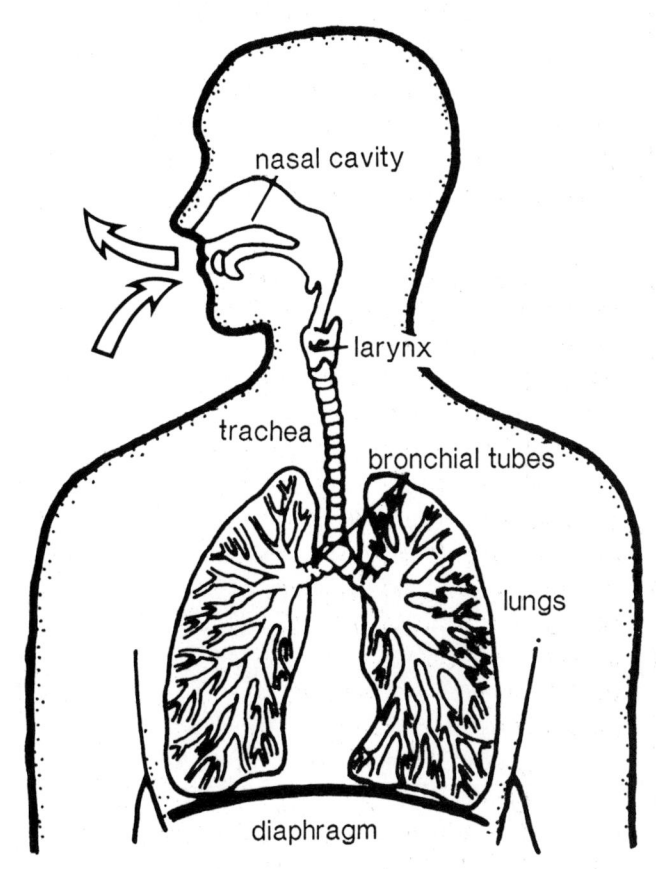

The air travels past the **epiglottis**, past the **larynx** and down the **trachea**, through the bronchial tubes and into the **lungs**.

Each **bronchial tube** (bronchi) branches out into a network of even smaller tubes (**bronchioles**), finally ending in air sacs, or **alveoli**. Air moves through these small passages and into the air sacs.

In the alveoli oxygen needed to maintain the body's cells is exchanged for the carbon dioxide the body has created as the cells used energy.

The oxygen is then carried by the blood to cells in the rest of the body. Here, oxygen can turn food into energy.

Exhaled air, laden with carbon dioxide, follows the same route out of the body.

Something To Do

1. Discover the breathing rate while performing the following activities. Ask a friend to time you while you count the number of breaths you take per minute for each activity, a) reading a book, b) walking, c) running, c) eating.

2. Tell how the respiratory system is related to the circulatory system, the nervous system, and the digestive system.

3. Write five questions that could be used in review of the respiratory system.

Air Flow

Read each block of information on the right. Cut out and glue each block in the correct order to show the complete respiratory process.

Respiratory Process

1.

2.

3.

4.

5.

6.

Inside each alveoli oxygen passes through the thin membrane into the bloodstream. In exchange, carbon dioxide passes out of the bloodstream and into the alveoli.

Laden with carbon dioxide, a waste product produced as cells use energy, the air is exhaled out of the body through the same channels it entered.

Each bronchial tube branches out into smaller tubes called bronchioles. At the end of each bronchiole, air is collected in an air sac, or alveoli.

Air flows past the epiglottis, beyond the larynx, down the trachea, and finally enters the lungs through the bronchial tubes.

Nose and mouth bring the air into the body with the help of the diaphragm muscles. The inhaled air is warmed, moistened, and cleaned of dirt and germs.

Having reached the bloodstream, the fresh oxygen travels to cells throughout the body. There it helps turns food nutrients into energy.

What is the one thing you must always remember to do before you exhale? To find out, write the first letter of each box above the corresponding number.

$$\overline{}_{4} \quad \overline{}_{1} \quad \overline{}_{5} \quad \overline{}_{2} \quad \overline{}_{6} \quad \overline{}_{3}$$

Chemical Test

Materials

drinking glass, straw, BTB (Bromthymol Blue) solution, sheet of paper

Procedure

1. Fill a drinking glass half full with BTB solution. Examine the solution's color.
2. Put a straw into the glass and exhale through it slowly. Blow your breath in the solution for 2-3 minutes. Examine the color change.
3. What is in your exhaled air that caused this color change? Do you know how to get it back to its original color?

Secret Passage

Prove to yourself that your nose, throat, ears and mouth are all connected by a secret passage by following these breathing tricks.

Procedure

1. Breathe in and out naturally through both of your nostrils. Keep mouth closed.
2. Breathe in and out using only one nostril. Use your finger to close the other nostril.
3. Breathe air in through one nostril and out the other nostril.
4. Pinch your nostrils closed so you can breathe through your mouth only.
5. Breathe air in through your mouth and out through your nose. Reverse it.
6. Pinch your nose closed and swallow. This closes the air passages to your ears. Let go of your nose and swallow again. This reopens the passages.

Make a Lung

Construct a working model of the lung.

Materials
a clear bottle with a lid, 1 large balloon, 1 small balloon, 2 rubber bands, 1 plastic straw, scissors or knife, small amount of clay or wax

Procedure
1. Punch a hole in the lid. Insert the plastic straw so it fits snugly and will not fall into the bottle.
2. Using scissors or knife, cut away the bottom of the bottle.
3. Snip the rounded end of the large balloon off. Lay it underneath the open end of the bottle. Pull the balloon up over the sides of the bottle. Secure tightly with a rubber band.
4. Attach the small balloon to the bottom of the straw with the rubber band.
5. Insert the straw and balloon into the bottle. Twist the lid on tightly. Secure all air leaks with a ring of clay or wax.
6. Push the balloon in at the base of the bottle. Feel the air rush out at the opposite end through the open end of the straw. The balloon lung should expand and relax with the change of space.

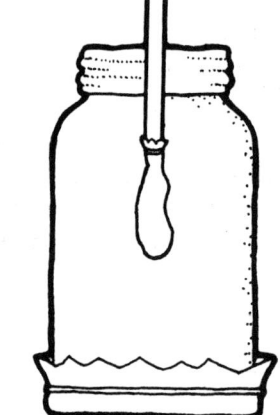

Lung Capacity

Measure your lung capacity with this experiment.

Materials
large glass or plastic jug, shallow pan, water, flexible plastic or rubber tubing, clean piece of glass tubing or plastic straw for each person performing the experiment

Procedure
1. Fill a large jug with water. Hold a hand over the opening and invert it in a partially filled pan of water.
2. Insert tubing into the mouth of the jug. Insert glass tube or plastic straw into the tubing.
3. Put tube into your mouth, take a big breath and exhale completely.

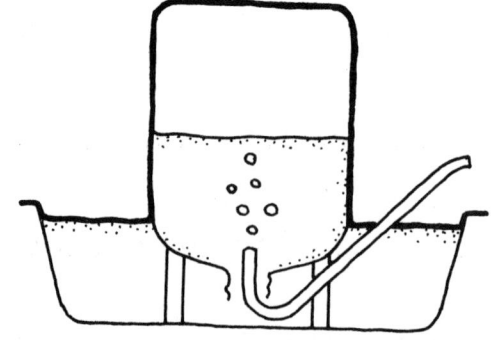

4. Measure the amount of water that was forced out of the jug by refilling it. This is your lung capacity.
5. Compare capacity before and after exercise.

1. Speech

Find out more about how humans make sounds and how these sounds combine to make speech. How does this compare with other animals?

2. Hic! Hic! Hiccup!

Coughing, sneezing, hiccuping, sighing, yawning, crying, and laughing are all unusual forms of respiration that occur in response to physical or emotional triggers. Find out why these involuntary responses happen and what their effects are.

3. Altitude Sickness

Research breathing problems people experience at high altitudes. Find out what is done about this problem when climbing high mountains, flying at high altitudes, or during space travel.

4. Pollutant Standards Index

One measurement of air quality is the concentration of dust or soot in the air. The Environmental Protection Agency (EPA) and the Council on Environmental Quality have developed the Pollutant Standards Index (PSI) to measure air quality. Find out more about this index and how pollutants are monitored.

5. Air Pollution

Research the effects of air pollution on the respiratory system. Find out where the term smog first originated, what causes smog, where is it most commonly located, and what effects it has on people, animals, and the environment.

6. No Smoking, Please

Tobacco smoking is a far greater health risk than most air pollution. Research the effects smoking has on a person's health, specifically, their respiratory system. What diseases are associated with smoking?

7. Researchers

The following people made important discoveries about the respiratory system. Choose one and research his contributions:
Joseph Black, Robert Boyle, John Mayow, Robert Hooke, Richard Lower, and Antonoine Lavoisier.

8. Respiratory Diseases

Research one of the diseases of the respiratory system. You could choose one of the following:
pneumonia, hay fever, bronchitis, pleurisy, cancer, tuberculosis, emphysema, or pneumoconiosis.
Discover the role the immune system plays on the inhalation of contaminants within the respiratory system.

1. Mouth–To–Mouth Resuscitation

Invite a trained rescuer (paramedic, fire fighter, nurse, or Red Cross volunteer) to demonstrate the process of mouth–to–mouth resuscitation and the Heimlich Maneuver. Make a list of questions to ask the life saving guest.

2. Breathe In – Breathe Out

Create a poster that shows the respiratory process.

3. Effects of Smoking

Educate others on the harmful effects of smoking through the presentation of a puppet show or skit.

4. There's A Difference

Create a collage or drawing showing the contrast between clean air and polluted air. Make a list of five suggestions for cleaning up polluted air.

5. Lifesaver Kit

Put together a box of information about the Heimlich Maneuver, mouth-to-mouth resuscitation, and safety measures that relate to respiration. Include brochures from organizations like the Red Cross, magazine articles, and self-made informational material.

6. Travel Agent

Pretend you are a travel agent for the internal systems of your body. Devise a travelogue (points of interest, itinerary, etc.) for a client of air who will be inhaled by you soon.

7. Crossword Puzzle

Create a crossword puzzle using the terms associated with the respiratory system.

8. Game

Design a game that takes participants on a trip through the respiratory system.

Name _____

Focus Page

I. Read each statement. Put a **T** on the blank for a true statement and an **F** for a false statement.

___ 1. Breathing is an involuntary process.

___ 2. The respiratory system helps produce sound.

___ 3. All the air that is inhaled is exhaled with each breath.

___ 4. Germs and dust particles are trapped in the nose by mucus.

___ 5. The pharynx is located below the epiglottis.

___ 6. The respiratory system does not coordinate with any other systems.

___ 7. Bronchial tubes bring air into the lungs.

___ 8. The exchange of gases takes place in the alveoli.

___ 9. The diaphragm is a muscle.

___ 10. Exhaled air is full of oxygen.

II. Read the descriptions in the column on the right. Find the term on the left that goes with each description. Write the correct letter on the blank next to each term.

___ 1. carbon dioxide   a. the mouth

___ 2. vocal cords   b. tissue folds in the larynx

___ 3. cilia   c. life-saving technique for a chocking victim

___ 4. respiration   d. muscle responsible for breathing

___ 5. pleural sac   e. a waste product of cell metabolism

___ 6. Heimlich Maneuver   f. tiny branches with air sacs at the end

___ 7. oral cavity   g. heart and lungs are located here

___ 8. diaphragm   h. the breathing process

___ 9. thorax   i. airtight lining of the lung

___ 10. bronchioles   j. tiny hairs in the nose move dirt out

Write the answers to the following questions and activities on a separate piece of paper.

III. Define these terms:
carbon dioxide   bronchial tubes   nose   epiglottis   alveoli

IV. Choose of the following to draw.
a. A diagram of the respiratory system. Label all the parts.
b. The interior of a lung. Show the exchange of gases.

V. Answer the following questions using concise, clear sentences.
a. Describe three of the four jobs the respiratory system does.
b. Discuss the two components of air that are a part of the respiratory system.
c. Explain how sound is made.
d. Explain the exchange of gases in the respiratory process. Why is it important?
e. What role does the diaphragm play in breathing?

Feed Me – I Am Yours

Every cell in your body needs fuel, or energy, to do its specific job. This fuel comes from the foods you eat. Food must be processed into chemical particles that cells in the body can use for metabolism and growth. When food enters the body, the **digestive system** swings into action to prepare food for absorbtion by cells so it can be turned into energy. Cells use both food and oxygen to release energy. The body needs an orderly way to carry nutrients to the cells when they need them and in a form they can use. The process that does this is the work of both the digestive system and the circulatory system.

The main parts of the digestive system are **oral cavity** (mouth, teeth, tongue, saliva glands, and pharynx), the **alimentary canal** (consisting of the **esophagus**, **stomach**, **small intestine**, **large intestine**, and **rectum**), as well as certain glands such as the **liver** and the **pancreas**. By working together, these organs break down food both mechanically and chemically. Breaking food into smaller pieces makes it easier for it to be transported and used by cells all over the body. One of the wonderful things about the human body is its ability to both store and distribute nutrients to all the cells according to their needs during periods of either high or low demand.

Once food is ingested, it is mechanically broken down by being mashed, chopped and churned into a thick mixture. Chemically, juices are mixed with this mixture to extract the nutrients and change them into basic elements the cells can use. Proteins are broken down into amino acids, carbohydrates become glucose, and fats becomes fatty acids and glycerol. These are all elements that cells can use.

Something To Do

1. Make a list of the main parts of the digestive system. Make your own drawing of the digestive system. Locate each part on your drawing by drawing a line from the listing to the drawing.

2. Explain why food has to be broken down into very small pieces.

3. Ask four good questions that could be answered by reading the material above.

4. Define metabolism.

Going Down

What happens to the food you eat? To begin with, food goes in the mouth. You bite the food with the front teeth and grind it with your back teeth. Small glands under the tongue release a watery liquid called **saliva**. Saliva makes the food soft, wet, and easier to chew. It also begins to chemically break down food with a special starch-to-sugar enzyme. Because the production of saliva is controlled by the autonomic nervous system, sometimes just thinking about some foods will trigger the body to produce saliva. This is the body's way of preparing itself to eat and digest food.

After the food has been chewed and mixed with saliva, the tongue pushes it to the very back of the mouth, the **pharynx**. Here there are two pipes. One (the **trachea**) is for air. It is critical that food gets into the correct tube, so when food is swallowed the **epiglottis** (a small flap at the base of the tongue) closes so that food doesn't enter the trachea.

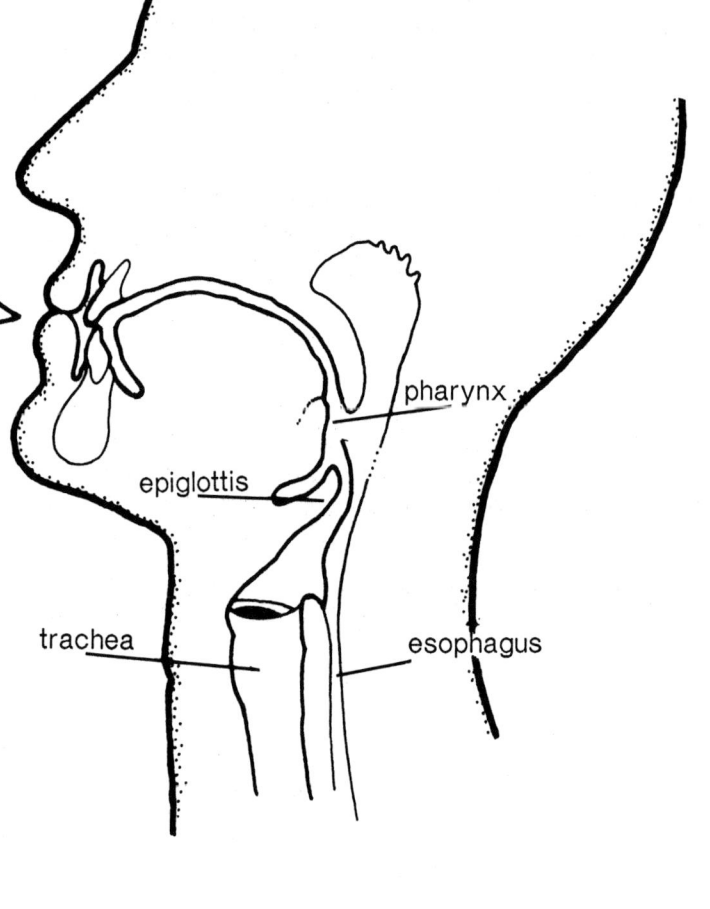

The other tube, the **esophagus**, is the food pipe. The esophagus, a long, muscular tube located behind the trachea, is used to push the chewed food down to the stomach. It is about ten inches long and is smaller in width than the trachea. The sides of the esophagus are strong and sturdy, yet flexible enough to push food down to the stomach. Strong, rhythmic, wave-like contractions of the walls of the esophagus, called **peristalsis**, move the food to the stomach. It can move food down to the stomach in as little as seven seconds. A valve-like muscle where the esophagus meets the stomach regulates how much food enters the stomach, so it doesn't all enter the stomach at the same time.

Something To Do

1. Explain the relationship of the trachea, epiglottis, and esophagus.
2. Make a diagram or flow chart that shows how food gets from your hand to your stomach.
3. Make a list of verbs that tell what happens to food from the time it enters the mouth until it leaves the stomach.
4. Circle the six words in bold type. Define each one.

You Are What You Eat

Healthy bodies need a variety of food substances called **nutrients**. Eating a variety of foods will provide the body's requirements of **proteins**, **carbohydrates** (sugar and starches), **fats**, **vitamins** and **minerals**.

Proteins are building blocks for the body. They are important for growth and development of all body tissue and the formation of hormones. Meat, fish, dairy products, eggs, nuts, seeds, whole grains, and beans are sources of proteins.

Carbohydrates (sugar and starches) are the chief source of energy for all bodily functions and assist in the digestion of other foods. Main sources of carbohydrates are cereals, bread, spaghetti, grains, fruits and vegetables, and potatoes.

Fats supply fuel, provide a layer of insulation against the cold, act as lubricants, and aid in the absorption of some vitamins. Fats take longer to digest, giving a full feeling for a longer period of time. Milk products, eggs, and oils are all fats of animal origin. Some fats are also derived from vegetables.

Vitamins and **Minerals** are needed in small quantities for chemical reactions in the body. **Vitamins** originally come from living things like plants and animals. They are important to a growing body. For example, vitamin A keeps skin and eyes healthy; vitamin C fights germs; and vitamin D keeps bones and teeth strong and sturdy. **Minerals** originally come from non-living things like rocks. They are extremely important to a healthy body, but are not needed in large amounts. Vitamins and minerals are found in many different foods.

The body needs nutrients to maintain itself. Different food substances work together to provide the body with what it needs to stay healthy and continue to grow. No one food or food group can supply all the necessary nutrients. The goal should be to eat a balanced diet that includes a variety of needed nutrients.

Something To Do

1. Consult a dictionary and write a definition of each nutrient listed.
2. List three items from the first three categories that you enjoy eating.
3. Research the recommended daily allowance for each nutrient.

Zooming Enzymes

The body can handle a variety of foods because it produces hormones in response to the type of food being digested. The hormones, in turn, control the release of enzymes as well as the movement of the food. **Enzymes** are proteins that act as catalysts in the chemical reactions in the body. Enzymes make things happen fast. They speed up chemical processes in the body to help produce energy and perform their special functions. There are over one thousand different kinds of enzymes in the body; each performing a specific job.

One enzyme, called **amylase**, is produced in the salivary glands. Its job is to help digest food. This enzyme of the mouth does two things:

1. Amylase begins the chemical breakdown of carbohydrates in food. This enzyme turns the starches found in the body into sugars used for energy. This sugar is called glucose.

2. Amylase also controls the amount of energy that enters the body's system. Too much energy at one time could cause problems.

Something To Do
Perform this simple experiment to discover for yourself how the enzyme amylase breaks starch down into sugars.

Materials
unsalted soda cracker, clock or timer

Procedure
1. Chew an unsalted soda cracker. Keep it in your mouth for five minutes.
2. Pay close attention to the taste changes in your mouth. Describe the change of taste that occurs in your mouth during that five minute chewing time.
3. What are the effects of saliva on the starchy soda cracker.
4. Try this experiment with other types of foods; a piece of bread, french fries.
5. Research more about glucose and how it is related to the digestive system.

Stomach

So far, the digestive system has involved the oral cavity, the salivary glands, and the esophagus. The real work of the digestive system begins in the stomach.

The stomach is a large, muscular sac that stores and digests food. It can expand like an elastic bag to hold up to 2 1/2 pints of food. It fits under the diaphragm on the left side of the abdomen, carefully shielded by the five lower ribs. Food usually stays in the stomach for two to six hours during digestion. Carbohydrates leave the stomach after a few hours. Proteins stay in the stomach longer, and fatty foods don't leave the stomach for many hours.

The walls of the stomach are lined with strong muscles to churn food around and around like a washing machine. These muscles contract and expand, mechanically digesting food. Special digestive juices, called **gastric juices**, pour in from the stomach walls after being stimulated by the smell or thought of food, by the arrival of food into the stomach, and by hormones. The juices mix together with the food while it is being churned. The gastric juices are composed of strong hydrochloric acid, a digestive enzyme called pepsin, and mucus. The acid and enzyme begin breaking down protein and kill bacteria, while the mucus forms a protective layer in the stomach to protect it from being burned by the acid.

The stomach consists of three layers of muscles, each contracting in a different direction. All of this pushing and pulling in various directions, churns food into a thick soup. At this point, stomach muscles are prepared to move the food toward the **duodenum**, or small intestine, for the next stage of digestion.

A **sphincter muscle** oversees the passage of digested food out of the stomach. Every few minutes, the sphincter muscle opens up, squeezing out small amounts of the food mixture into the small intestine. The sphincter closes until the small intestine is prepared to receive more food rather than to receive food at the rate it is eaten.

Something To Do

1. Circle the key words on this page. Briefly define each.

2. Everyone has listened to their stomach rumble during digestion. These rumblings come from all of the muscular activity and pouring of juices within the digestive system. Imagine these rumblings as understandable conversation between your digestive parts. Prepare a dialogue between some of the digestive characters that reflects your knowledge of the digestive system.

3. Briefly explain what happens to food from the time it enters the stomach until it exits.

Small Intestine

The food processed in the stomach moves slowly into the small **intestine**, continuing its journey through the digestive system. Most of the digestion and absorbtion of food takes place in the small intestine. The small intestine is by no means small. It is a long tube that winds itself through the digestive tract. If stretched from top to bottom, it would be taller than a football goal post. It is about 21 to 24 feet long.

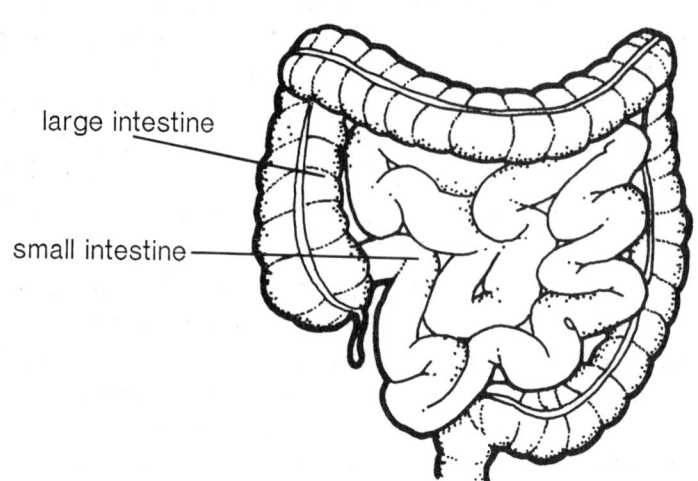

large intestine

small intestine

The first section of the small intestine is the **duodenum**. It is a C-shaped piece about a foot long. Here the food mixture from the stomach is mixed with digestive juices from the pancreas and liver. The enzymes in the juices from the pancreas aid in the breakdown of carbohydrates, fats, and protein into forms cells can use. The liver produces a thick green liquid called **bile**. Bile assists in the digestion of fats. It is stored in the **gallbladder** until the duodenum needs it.

The middle section of the small intestine is called the **jejunum**, and the last section is called the **ileum**. Partly digested food from the duodenum makes its way to these two areas for more intense chemical breakdown and absorbtion into the blood stream. Food that was delivered from the stomach is turned into a thin, watery liquid by the extra juices from the jejunum and ileum. After hours of digestion, food particles are small enough to be absorbed into the bloodstream.

If the walls of the small intestine were smooth, the flow of this food would be so quick that the body would not have enough time to absorb all the nutrients it needs. However, the walls of the small intestine are filled with hundreds of folds and are lined with millions of tiny, finger-like bumps called **villi** that increase the absorptive surface of the intestine five times more than what it would be if it were smooth. The villi pick up nutrients from the liquified food and send them into lymph vessels or to the capillaries to be absorbed by the blood. From here the absorbed nutrients travel through the bloodstream to the liver, the body's largest internal organ where the nutrients are filtered, processed and then distributed to all parts of the body.

Something To Do

1. Underline a least five key facts or concepts from the information above. Use these ideas in a summary paragraph of the material.

2. Cut a 24 foot piece of string. Fold it to fit on this page.

3. Place a quarter of a slice of bread, spoonful of peanut butter, spoonful of jelly, an apple slice and a cookie into separate bowls with 3 tablespoons of water. Mash each with a fork. Determine which foods are digested easily and which ones will need additional juices to help in their breakdown.

Leftovers

Cows and horses are able to survive on the grasses they eat because their digestive system is equipped to handle them. People cannot. The human body cannot digest cellulose, the fibrous or shredded carbohydrate found in grass and plant foods. Some researchers claim that the appendix (which is of no use to humans at all) once served the purpose of digesting such roughage many years ago when humans did consume heavy fiber foods such as bark. Daily consumption of fiber or roughage is important, though. It aids in the process of peristalsis and prevents constipation. Fresh vegetables, fruits, whole-grain breads and cereals, are excellent sources of daily fiber.

The food particles the body cannot digest continue to travel from the stomach, through the small intestine, and into the **large intestine**. The large intestine is much wider than the small intestine and also much shorter. It is only five feet long and is shaped like an upside down letter U. Inside the large intestine, the indigestible food particles and water are recycled for the last time to remove any nutrients and water and send them into the bloodstream. The non-usable food becomes dry and solid. It is stored here in the large intestine until enough has been collected to be eliminated through the rectum.

On the average, the entire digestive process takes about 20 to 25 hours. The actual rate depends on several factors like what food is eaten, how much fat is eaten (fat slows the process), and the temperature of food (cold food like ice cream slows the system). Here is a possible timetable of the digestion process:

  oral cavity – few seconds to a
  couple of minutes
  esophagus – 10 seconds
  stomach – 2-4 hours
  small intestine – up to 5 hours
  large intestine – 12-36 hours
      depending on the type of food eaten

Something To Do

1. Calculate your own digestive process.
   - When did you last eat a meal?
   - When will your stomach be almost empty?
   - At what time will there still be food in your small intestines?
   - When will the food energy be travelling in your blood to all parts of your body?
   - Is there ever a time during your 24 hour day when you have completely digested all of your food? If so, during what hours?

2. Find out more about the appendix.

3. Discover the differences between our digestive process and that of a cow or horse.

Gulp

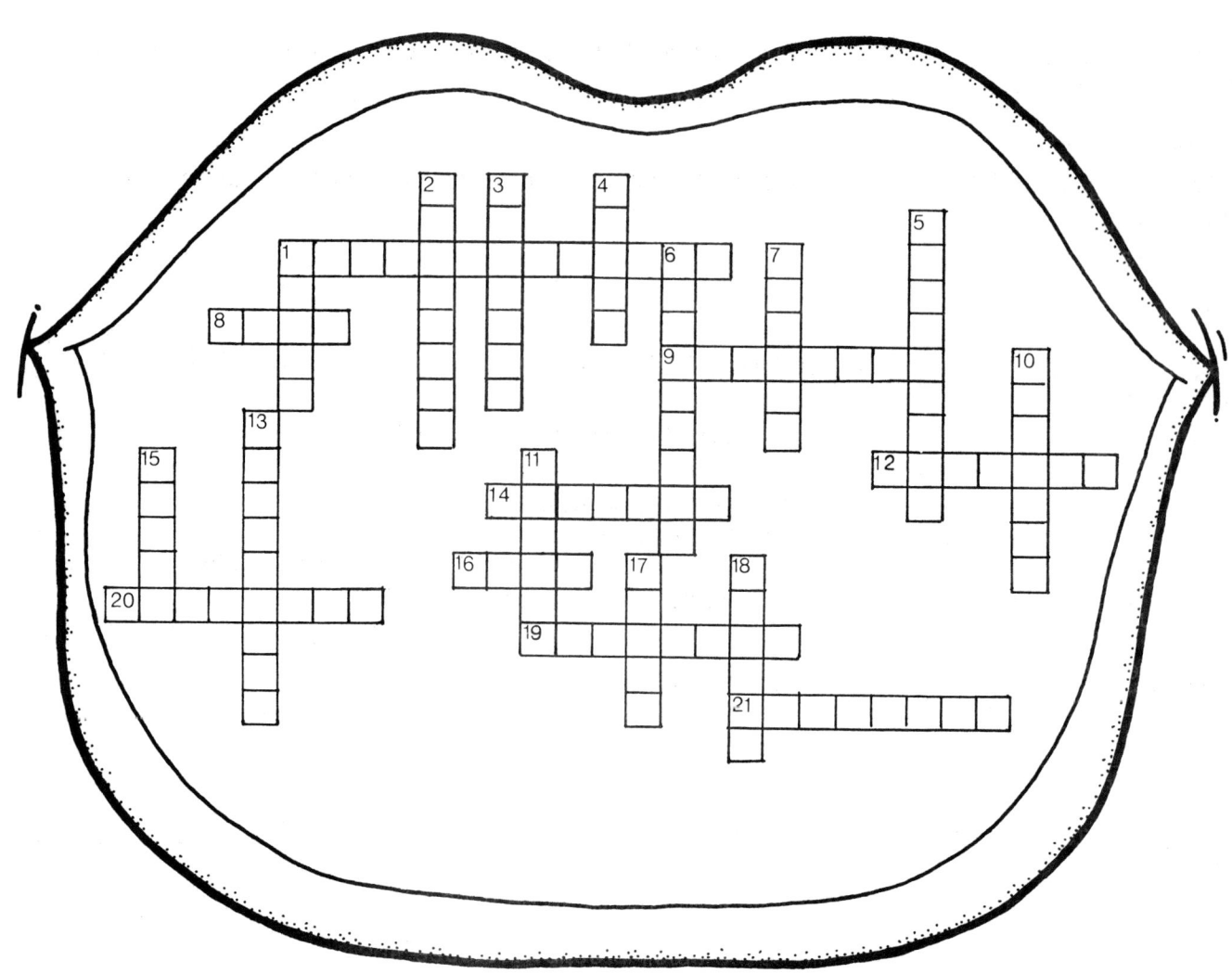

Across

1. ____ are foods containing sugars and starches.
8. The liver produces this thick green liquid to help digest foods.
9. Juices from this organ help breakdown carbohydrates, fats, and proteins.
12. These speed up the body's chemical processes.
14. Name for the middle section of the small intestine.
16. Milk products are energy foods consisting mainly of ____.
19. Essential elements that come from non-living things like rocks.
20. Foods considered to be the building blocks for the body.
21. Essential food elements that come from living things like plants and animals.

Down

1. Food combines with oxygen to provide ____ with energy.
2. The C-shaped section of small intestine.
3. An enzyme produced by the salivary gland.
4. The ____ intestine is over 20 feet long.
5. The large ____ takes care of non-digested food.
6. Another name for the food pipe.
7. Gastric ____ chemically break down food.
10. Has three layers of muscles to churn food into a thick soup.
11. Non-usable food particles are eliminated through the ____.
13. Eating a balanced diet will provide the body with essential ____.
15. The pancreas and ____ secrete gastric juices.
17. Name for the final section of the small intestine.
18. Liquid that begins chemically breaking down food in the mouth.

Enzyme Time

Stomach cells secrete a solution of hydrochloric acid and an enzyme called pepsin to aid in the breakdown of food.

Materials
5 test tubes, pepsin solution, water, hydrochloric acid, egg white (cooked), source of heat for boiling, eyedropper

Procedure
1. Fill 5 test tubes 1/4 full of water.
2. Place a small piece of cooked egg white into each one. All egg pieces should be the same size.
3. Number the test tubes 1 through 5 and add the following ingredients:

   test tube 1 – nothing
   test tube 2 – 10 drops of 10% hydrochloric acid
   test tube 3 – 2 drops of 1% pepsin solution
   test tube 4 – 2 drops of 1% pepsin and 10 drops of 10% hydrochloric acid
   test tube 5 – same as 4, but bring solution to a boil

4. Place test tubes in a warm place.
5. Observe any changes after 24 hours. Only one tube will begin digestion. Which one? Why?

Starch Test

Materials
unsalted soda cracker, water, test tube, eyedropper, iodine, various foods (popcorn, banana, carrot, cheese)

Procedure
1. Fill the test tube with 10 milliliters of water.
2. Place a few cracker crumbs in test tube.
3. Add 10 drops of iodine and shake.
4. If starch is present, the mixture will turn dark blue or black.
5. Repeat with other food items.
6. Record and report the results.

Sweet as Sugar

Materials

3 milliliters of saliva, water, test tube, unsalted cracker crumbs, Benedict's solution, source of heat for boiling, eyedropper

Procedure

1. Collect saliva in test tube.
2. Add 3 ml. water with eyedropper.
3. Add a few cracker crumbs.
4. Warm the test tube to body temperature by holding it in your hand for 10 minutes.
5. Add 5 ml. Benedict's solution.
6. Heat the test tube until it boils gently.
7. If sugar is present, a red-orange mist will develop.

Sugar Test

Materials

saucepan, source of heat for boiling, Benedict's solution, various foods (apple, lettuce, carrots, squash, sweet potato, etc.)

Procedure

1. Partially cook the fruits and vegetables in a little water. Mash each separately.
2. Add Benedict's solution and boil.
3. Observe the changes. If sugar is present, a red-orange mist will develop. Which foods contain sugar?

Testing for Fat

Materials
3 inch squares of brown paper bag, various foods (butter, boiled egg white and yolk, peanuts, apple, bread, hot dog, cheese, etc.), light

Procedure
1. Cut up squares from the brown paper bag.
2. Rub a piece of food on the paper.
3. Let it dry.
4. Hold it up to a light. If fat is present, the light will show through the paper square.

Discovery Experiment

Testing for Proteins

Materials
5% copper sulfate solution, eyedropper, 1 tablespoon of lime, 2 jars, cup, water, various foods (carrots, cheese, meat, peanut butter, cooked egg slice, etc.)

Procedure
1. Make a 5% solution of copper sulfate in one jar.
2. Make a second solution by dissolving a tablespoon of lime into a cup of water.
3. Add equal amounts of these two solutions to various foods with eyedropper.
4. If a violet color appears, then protein is present.

Enzymes

The body turns starch into glucose (a type of sugar) so it can be used by the cells. Enzymes found in saliva and in the intestines speed up the conversion process. In this experiment you will test for the conversion of starch to sugar when mixed with an enzyme found in saliva.

You will be testing for starch or sugar using iodine and Benedict's solution. Iodine indicates the presence of starch by turning a dark blue color. Benedict's solution indicates the presence of simple sugars by turning the substance being tested colors that range from blue to yellow to red, depending on the concentration of sugar.

Materials

hot plate, beaker, water, iodine solution, starch*, Benedict's solution, medicine dropper, saliva, six test tubes (numbered from 1 to 6)

> * Soak two handfuls of oat cereal (not instant) in 500 milliliters of water for 20 minutes. Mash and mix occasionally. Use the milky liquid on top for this experiment. Or prepare a thin cornstarch solution by mixing a tablespoon of cornstarch with a cup of water and heating for a few minutes.

Procedure

1. Fill a small beaker with water and place it on a hot plate to boil. This will be used for a hot water bath.
2. Put 2 milliliters of starch water in test tube 1. Add two drops of iodine solution and gently shake it. Wait one minute. Check the color. Save this tube.
3. Put 2 milliliters of starch in test tube 2. Add 2 milliliters of Benedict's solution. Place it in the hot water bath for five minutes. Watch the color change. Save this tube.
4. Add one milliliter of saliva to test tube 3. Add two drops of iodine solution and mix gently. Watch the color change. Save this tube.
5. Add one milliliter of saliva to test tube 4. Add two milliliters of Benedict's solution and mix gently. Heat tube in water bath for five minutes. Watch color change. Save tube.
6. Add one milliliter of saliva and one dropper of starch to test tube 5. Mix gently. Let stand for five minutes (very important). After five minutes, add two drops of iodine solution. Check the color.
7. Add one milliliter of saliva and one dropper of starch to test tube 6. Add two milliliters of Benedict's solution. Mix and heat in a hot water bath for five minutes. Watch color change.

Complete the following chart and explain the results of the experiment.

test tube	mixture	color change	represents
1	starch, iodine		
2	starch, Benedict's		
3	saliva, iodine		
4	saliva, Benedict's		
5	saliva, starch, iodine		
6	saliva, starch, Benedict's		

1. Fuel Food

There are two ways living things get fuel. One way is to produce their own food internally using the light from the sun; the other way involves eating other living things. Only plants are able to produce their own food by using sunlight. Find out more about this energy-producing method by researching the process of photosynthesis.

2. Digestive Duties

The digestive system is a very complex system. The following is a list of terms associated with the digestive process. Discover more about these things and the role they play in the digestion of food.

amino acids	glucose	duodenum
sphincter	peristalsis	alimentary canal
liver	pancreas	bile
gall bladder	villi	

3. Ulcers

Discover what an ulcer is and how it originates. What can be done to prevent one?

4. Stomach Aches

Sometimes eating food, even good food, can make you feel bad. Find out why you get stomach aches.

5. Food and Drug Administration

Contact your local FDA office. Request materials about food from them that you would be interested in sharing with your class.

6. Balanced Diet

Find out what a well-balanced diet is and why it is so important. Based on this information, decide if your diet is well-balanced.

7. Dieting

How healthy is dieting? Research the pros and cons of fad dieting. Collect three or more diets. Compare and contrast them. Find evidence to support or refute the soundness or effectiveness of the diets.

8. Teeth

Teeth are the important first step of the digestive process. Find out as much as you can about these useful utensils. Find out why you have different kinds of teeth, what each kind is used for, and what you can do to take care of them.

1. How Much Food?

The average person eats three pounds of food daily or about 1,095 pounds of food per year. Calculate the amount of food you and your family have already consumed since January 1st. A sanitation truck averages 20,000 pounds per load. How many truckloads will you have consumed in one year?

2. Look at Me Eat

Create a collage of people eating. Include pictures of various foods that you like. Arrange the collage onto a shape of something associated with food.

3. Digestive Drawing

Draw a diagram of the digestive system on a large piece of poster board. Label each of its parts and briefly summarize their functions. Color each part a different color.

4. Take A Trip

Imagine yourself as a travel agent planning a trip for the cookie you are about to eat for a snack. Develop an itinerary or guidebook for your client. Set departure and arrival times.

5. Flow Chart

Design a flow chart or roller movie of the digestive process.

6. FDA

Invite a representative from the local chapter of the Food and Drug Administration to talk to you about food and how this organization monitors food standards.

7. Recipe Book

Compile a collection of favorite healthy recipes into a book to share with your friends.

8. Project Cube

Make a project cube that shows information about the digestive system. On each side of the cube put a picture and description of a different part of the system. Number each picture to indicate the order it relates to in the digestive process.

Name _____

Focus Page

I. Fill in the blanks with one of the words listed below.

digestive   esophagus   nutrients   small   minerals
carbohydrates   muscles   enzymes   mouth   large

1. _____ speed up the chemical reactions in the body.

2. _____ , sugars and starches, are a body's fuel food.

3. The stomach consists of three layers of _____ .

4. The _____ intestine treats indigestible food particles.

5. Food is turned into nutrients cells can use to make energy by the
_____ process.

6. Eating a balanced diet will provide the body with essential _____ .

7. The _____ is a part of the oral cavity where the digestive process starts.

8. The _____ forces food into the stomach by muscular action.

9. _____ originally came from non-living things like rocks.

10. Most of the digestion and absorbtion of food takes place in the
_____ intestine.

II. Read each statement. Write a **T** on the blank for a true statement and a **F** for a false statement.

____ 1. The body can store and distribute nutrients to cells throughout the body.

____ 2. The esophagus is the food pipe.

____ 3. Peristalsis takes place in the trachea.

____ 4. Proteins are not essential for growth.

____ 5. The digestive process mechanically and chemically breaks down food.

____ 6. Enzymes are produced in the salivary glands.

____ 7. Gastric juices aid in chemically breaking down food in the stomach.

____ 8. The duodenum, jejunum and ileum are parts of the small intestine.

____ 9. The villi found in the walls of the small intestine increase absorbtion of food.

____ 10. Non-usable foods are recycled until they can be used by the body.

Focus Page, continued

Put the answers to these questions and activities on a separate piece of paper.

III. Define the following terms.

saliva   nutrients   stomach   villi   esophagus

IV. Choose one of the following to draw.

    a. A diagram of the digestive system. Label each part.

    b. Name the nutrients that are essential to a balanced diet. Draw at least three items for each category and label each item.

V. Answer the following questions using clear, concise sentences.

    a. What is the function of the digestive system?

    b. Explain the process of digestion.

    c. Define a balanced diet.

    d. Food stays in the small intestine longer than in the stomach. Give two reasons for this.

    e. How is the digestive system linked to the circulatory system?

Answers

The following are possible answers for some of the questions in the **Something To Do** sections and the **Focus Pages**. Where answers vary depending on personal choices, no answers are given.

Page 4
1. 12 pints, 24 cups, 384 tablespoons
2. Transportation of essential nutrients, hormones and oxygen to cells, remove wastes, move blood through body
3. Circulate means to move or flow in a circle or circuit. Circuit is a closed path or route. The circulatory system moves blood through a closed path around the body.
4. approximately 70 beats per minute

Page 5
1. Answers will vary but could include hematology, hematologist, hematite, hematoma, hemoglobin, hemophilia, hemorrhage
2. Transports oxygen to all cells, transports antibodies to fight infection, carries food nutrients to the cells transports hormones, regulates water in tissue, equalizes heat in the body, produces clotting factors.

Page 6
1. Hemoglobin is important because it enables blood to carry oxygen to the cells.
2. Red blood cells have no nucleus and they cannot reproduce as white cells can. They perform different functions.

Page 7
2. Gradually introducing foreign substances into the body will gradually make it immune to their harmful effects.

Page 8
1. Answers can vary, but possible answers are:
   Red blood cells – transports oxygen, produced in spongy marrow of long bones, does not have a nucleus, removes carbon dioxide from cells.

   White blood cells – larger than red cells, fewer in the body than red cells, attacks harmful viruses or bacteria, three types, have no real shape.

   Plasma – yellow liquid in blood, 90% water, carries other cells.

   Platelets – bits of cells, helps blood clot, short life.
4. hemorrhage – severe or heavy bleeding

Page 9
2. Located in the center of the chest between the lungs, the heart is about the size of a large orange and weighs less than a pound. The tough muscle that forms its exteriors shape works continually to pump blood.
3. The cardiac muscle needs more nourishment because it works continually. It is the hardest working muscle in the body.

Page 11
1. approximately 160 miles per day
2. begins in right ventricle – lungs (picks up oxygen and deposits carbon dioxide) – enters left atrium – travels to left ventricle and into body's arteries and capillaries – travels around the body taking oxygen and food to cells and picking up wastes – returns to heart via veins – enters right atrium – returns to right ventricle

Page 14
1. Both the weight lifter and sprinter are involved in quick, physically exerting activities requiring a burst of energy over a short amount of time. Swimmers and long distance runners condition their hearts and breathing processes to withstand longer terms of physically exertion, thus increasing their heart and lung capacity.

Focus Pages, pgs. 25-26
1. j		1. supply
2. f		2. hemoglobin
3. i		3. heart
4. e		4. receive
5. a		5. veins
6. g		6. transportation
7. c		7. capillaries
8. b		8. valves
9. d		9. infection
10. h		10. needs

chambers – There are four chambers to the heart. The top two chambers, the left and right atria, receive blood returning from the heart. The bottom two chambers, the left and right ventricles, pump blood out of the heart, either to the lungs or to the body.

pacemaker – A small area of specialized nerve tissue that enables all four chambers of the heart to work together. It communicates with the brain to keep the heart beating at the proper rate.

plasma – This yellowish liquid in blood allows for the transportation of red cells, white cell,s platelets, hormones, and vitamins throughout the body. It is 90% water.

pulse – This is the consistent sound of the valves opening and closing in the heart. The valves make sure the blood flows in one direction only.

white blood cells – These cells fight infection. They are larger than red cells but are not as numerous. They have no color and no real shape and live for only 13 to 20 days.

See illustrations on pages 11 and 12.

a. See worksheet entitled **It's Just Blood**
b. Red cells are smaller than white cells but have no nucleus. Red cells carry oxygen to every cell in the body and take the waste product carbon dioxide to the lungs where it can be exhaled. White cells fight infection. Red cells live for 120 days, white cells only 13-20 days. Red cells are more numerous than white cells. White cells can reproduce, red cells cannot.
c. The right ventricle pumps blood to the lungs where it picks up oxygen and eliminates the waste, carbon dioxide. The blood then flows to the right atrium at the top of the heart, goes to the left ventricle and is pumped to every part of the body. While travelling through the body, the blood collects food nutrients from the intestines and delivers them to the cells where they are used with the oxygen to produce energy. The blood then comes back to the heart through the right atrium. It then goes into the right ventricle and is pumped to the lungs.
d. Arteries are the largest of the blood vessels. They carry the blood away from the heart. Capillaries are the smallest type of blood vessels. They are found all over they body, bringing oxygen and nutrients to every cell. Veins take the blood back to the heart.
e. Answers may vary but should include eating a well-balanced diet, getting exercise, reducing high blood pressure, not smoking, and eating a low fat/ low cholesterol diet.

Page 27
2. The respiratory center is responding to the excessive amount of carbon dioxide in the blood and signaling the body to get more oxygen.
3. The respiratory center is important because it controls the rate of breathing. Without this monitor, the body would not be able to take in extra amount of oxygen when it needs it (as during physical exertion) and cells would not get enough oxygen to be able to perform their jobs.

Page 28

1. The respiratory system is important because it brings oxygen into the body. This is needed by all cells to burn food to create energy. Once the food has been burned to create energy, the respiratory system along with the circulatory system is able to take the waste out of the body. Without this system, waste would build up and cells would be unable to function.
3. Brings oxygen into the body, take carbon dioxide out of the body, helps produce sound, maintain the acid level.

Page 29

1. A baby takes more breaths because at this stage of development, it needs more energy for cell growth and reproduction. Also because a baby's lungs are smaller, it cannot take as much air into the lungs with each breath as an adult.

Page 30

1. It cleans, moistens, and warms air.
2. The nose does a better job of cleaning, moistening, and warming the air than the mouth.
3. Some people theorize that nose shapes have developed in response to the need to filter and condition air that enters the body. A long thin nose would allow the air to stay in the nose longer and, thus, be most useful in a cold, dry climate. A short broad nose, however, would not allow the air a very long time to be filtered and warmed. This type of nose might be better suited for warm, moist climate.
4. The nose becomes red because of the amount of blood in the nose tissue. The blood is present to warm the air entering the nose.

Page 31

1. Answers should mention that this Is a life-saving technique whereby the rescuer stands behind the victim, places a fist just under the rib cage and gives quick upward thrusts to dislodge the food in the trachea.
4. Answers will vary but should indicate that when food or liquid is approaching the epiglottis closes off the trachea and opens the esophagus.

Page 32

1. Exhaled air travels from the lungs up the trachea. As it passes the vocal cords, they vibrate. The vibrations make sound waves.

Page 33

1. Air travels down the trachea into one of the two bronchial tubes before entering the lungs. The air continues into the smaller tubes called bronchioles. At the end of each tiny tube is an air sac, called alveoli. The air enters the sac that is in close contact with blood flowing through the capillaries. Oxygen crosses over the thin membrane into the bloodstream. In exchange, carbon dioxide crosses the membrane from the bloodstream to the air sac where it is then exhaled.
2. Any analogy that presents the image of branching.
3. The air sacs have a greater surface area where oxygen and carbon dioxide can pass through the surface. With a smaller surface area, the body would not be able to absorb enough oxygen to provide for its needs.

Page 34

1. The diaphragm muscles facilitate inhalation and exhalation. The muscles move downward and together, allowing the ribs to lift and air to enter the lungs. As the muscles relax, they move up, the ribs return to their normal position, and you exhale.
3. The diaphragm muscle is involuntary. We can control the rhythm at times, but it continues to work on its own.

Page 35

2. The respiratory system is related to other systems in the body because it involves organs such as the heart (pumps the blood through the body carrying the oxygen to the cells), the brain (controls the amounts of oxygen and carbon dioxide in the body), and many parts of the digestive system (oxygen combines with food to create energy).

Page 36

1. Nose
2. Air
3. Each
4. Inside
5. Having
6. Laden
Inhale

Focus Pages, pgs. 43–44

1. T
2. T
3. F
4. T
5. F
6. F
7. T
8. T
9. T
10. F

1. e
2. b
3. j
4. h
5. i
6. c
7. a
8. d
9. g
10. f

carbon dioxide – Exhaled air contains more carbon dioxide than oxygen. Carbon dioxide is a waste produce of cell metabolism.

bronchial tubes – Branching out from the base of the trachea are two stiff branches called bronchial tubes. They are surrounded by protective cartilage rings and expand or decrease in size with inhalation or exhalation. They branch into even smaller tubes after entering the lungs.

nose – The nose is the primary organ for bringing air into the body. It not only cleans the air coming in, but it also warms and moistens it.

epiglottis – Located atop the trachea, the epiglottis opens and closes itself to accommodate for food or air. A lid, the epiglottis opens for air and closes for food.

alveoli – Found at the end of each bronchiole within the lung, these tiny air sacs permit the exchange of oxygen for carbon dioxide during the breathing process.

See illustrations on pages 28 and 33.

a. The respiratory system performs several things for the body. It brings oxygen into the body to be absorbed and taken to cells to be used as energy, takes carbon dioxide from blood and expels it by exhaling, helps make sounds for speech, regulates the balance of acid in the blood.
b. Air is composed of oxygen, carbon dioxide and nitrogen. The most important element is oxygen. The amount of nitrogen inhaled and exhaled remains about the same, but 4% more carbon dioxide is exhaled than inhaled, and 4% more oxygen is inhaled than exhaled.
c. Air is exhaled out of the lungs. As it ascends through the trachea, the air rushes past the larynx, located on top of the trachea. Small tissue folds in the larynx, called vocal cords, vibrate with the air. The vibrations make sound waves.
d. Air is inhaled and travels down into the lungs ending up in tiny sacs called alveoli. The oxygen in the sac passes through the sac's thin walls and enters the bloodstream to be taken to the body's cells. As the oxygen passes into the bloodstream, the carbon dioxide passes into the alveoli sac and is then exhaled from the body. This exchange allows the body to cleanse itself regularly while still providing its cells with the oxygen needed to produce energy.
e. The muscle that permits the breathing process to continue is the diaphragm. To inhale, the diaphragm must move downward, allowing the ribs to rise and the lungs to fill with air. When the diaphragm relaxes, the ribs return to their normal position and air flows out of the lungs.

Page 45

2. Food must be broken down into small pieces because eventually it must be small enough to pass through the walls of the capillaries to the bloodstream where it is carried to all cells and used to create energy.
4. Metabolism is the physical and chemical process that allows cells to turn food nutrients and oxygen into energy.